"I met John at a church plant. ago and we roomed together. We talked until 2:00 a.m. one night, and John shared some of the most wonderful stories about God's love, power, and faithfulness. Since then we have taken summer missionary trips with youth together in south Texas and in Omaha. Working together with him has given me an amazing opportunity to see that the stories that John shares are so real. When you give your heart to God one hundred percent and sacrifice for God's mission, like John does, you can help people who struggle with all kinds of issues."
—Pastor Daniel Rodriguez
Iglesia Agua Viva, Omaha, Nebraska

"In his walk with Jesus, John Langer has demonstrated a giant faith because of his strong and robust devotional life. This book will be highly uplifting and motivating for many people. It will impact their lives, increase their knowledge, and show them the grace of the Lord Jesus Christ. I recommend it without any reservation and hope that it will contribute to the spiritual growth of each person who reads it."
—Pastor Rafael Nunez
Mission Mennonite Brethren Church, Mission, TX

"John is a man of amazing faith. His compassion and zeal for God and His people often brings him to tears. John is the finest example I know of a small town rural man making himself available for God to do extraordinary things in his life at home and on his travels throughout the world. His stories of God at work are incredible."
—Pastor Stephen Stout
Faith Bible Curch, Omaha, Nebraska

"John Langer moves on a daily basis with a keen sense of living his life in the empowering presence of God. This has given him a full understanding and acceptance of why God created him as He has. Add to this his deep desire to be obedient to the call of the Lord in every detail of life, and you can see why John is being used effectively. It is an inspiration to see God at work in and through his life."
—Pastor Dick Nickel
Rapid City, South Dakota

"When John shared stories of God's amazing healing and power and love that he witnessed on a mission trip to Africa, it renewed my faith in God and His love for us. This book is about God's power and love for those who believe in Jesus. John has a heart like David's and is willing to do whatever God asks him to do."
—Pastor Val Rush
Viborg United Methodist Church, Canton, South Dakota

"These accounts of God's moving thru John Langer attest to his prayerful preparation and his availability to the harvest. For those who are waiting on God to give them a wake up call, let this book be another one He has sent your way. Thank you, John, for this recap of what God has done and can do through a prepared and available servant."
—Pastor Kamalei Mark Teves
aloha.chapels@gmail.com

Yes, God Does Speak

John Langer

Mobile, Alabama

ISBN 978-1-58169-648-6
For Worldwide Distribution
Printed in the U.S.A.

Evergreen Press
P.O. Box 191540 • Mobile, AL 36619
800-367-8203

CONTENTS

ACKNOWLEDGMENTS

A special thanks to God the Father, Jesus Christ, and the Holy Spirit. Without them, this book would not be possible.

Thanks to my wife, Jill, who has been my beautiful bride of over 30 years; and my mom, Hazel, who has loved me unconditionally always and taught me how to love.

A big thank you goes out to Justine Garza, my daughter, who years ago asked me to please write down my stories to help my future grandchildren know God.

This book would not have happened if not for the encouragement of my sons, son-in-law, and their wives. Blessings to you always: James and Jaymi Langer, Jacob and Brianna Langer, Joshua Langer, Aaron Garza, and my two grandsons, Jackson and Ezra Langer.

Thanks also to Keith Carroll, my literary agent, who has helped me immensely; and thank you, Evergreen Press, for making this even a possibility.

Thanks also to my heavenly Father for giving me my dad, Duane, who passed away a few years back. He would have loved this book.

And finally to you readers who have chosen this book out of many: may you be blessed as you read my stories and may you know for yourself that . . .

Yes, God Does Speak!

INTRODUCTION

As I visit and share my stories of God, almost every person I share them with says the same thing, "John, you need to write a book." That has been a confirmation for me to write these stories down for you to read about how awesome our God truly is.

After sitting down and visiting with someone who asked me a question one day, a story came to mind that would help them understand the answer better, so I told it. As time went on, that has happened thousands of times. The life experiences God has brought me through have taught me much and have become a valuable gift from God.

Through the years God has given me some special times that I would keep track of in a daily journal, and now they are in this book for you to read.

For some of you, that fact may be enough to put this book down and walk away, but for others I hope it grabs your attention and moves you to read the words written here for you, in hopes you too will hear the voice of God.

You may not understand why you are even considering reading this book. You may think you have God's Word and that is enough. Well, God's Word is perfect and complete, but as Jesus told the disciples, "There is much more to tell you, but you are not ready." There are things He still wants to say to you, personally.

The stories written here are from a journey I have taken thus far, and my hope is that they will help you on your journey with God as well.

As you turn the pages, there will be touching stories that may move you to serve God in ways you weren't expecting or they may teach you there is a real enemy who is against you and that there is an answer to fighting and winning against that enemy.

You will be shown how God knows the future of your life down to the very smallest detail, and He wants you to have success in the plan He has for you.

There are places in this book where you will have to pause and ask: *Is that really true or is it even possible,* yet in the end my hope is that it will affect your life in a way that is both positive and life-changing.

As you read these stories may they touch your heart and give you a better understanding of God that will help you walk closer to Him. May the stories you read inspire you to pursue God with all your heart.

THE STORIES

Have you ever wondered if God still speaks today? Well the answer is *Yes, He does!*

As you read the stories in this book of just how awesome our heavenly Father is, one of the things I hope you take away from them is that God has not only spoken to me and many others, but that He will also speak to you and probably already has.

Many people come up to me after hearing that statement and say, "Well, just how does He speak to you? Is it through His Word or through prayer? Does He speak to you audibly or is it a gentle whisper in your mind? Does He speak through other believers or is it through the Holy Spirit living inside you?"

The answer again is, Yes He does. He does speak to us in all these ways and more. I hope by the end of this book you will have been able to grasp that God is much more than you ever thought He was.

These stories will challenge you and your walk with God. They will help you to rethink how incredibly fantastic is the God we serve. If you don't know God yet, you will get a glimpse of what some people have experienced in their walk with Him.

God has sent me to Thailand, Nepal, Burkina Faso, India, and other countries around the world where He has shown me wonderful people, places, and miracles that I would not have seen otherwise.

When I say God sent me, I am saying He told me to go, He spoke to me about it, and He guided me there. This does not in any way take away from the value of God's written Word; it only shows us that when He has a plan for us, sometimes He will share it with us step by step.

As I read my Bible each morning, I learn more and more about the Father, His Son, and the Holy Spirit. The verses and the lessons I learn have been more valuable than any other words spoken to me, so why would God still speak to me?

The reason is there is no place in the Bible that says, "John, go to India"; or "John, give all your money away." There are verses that say to go to all the places on earth, and Jesus did tell a man to sell all he had and give it all away, but that was not specific to the path God has for us individually.

Once I was sent by God to a place where a gun was put to my head, and another time I was on a plane that landed unexpectedly when the engine quit. God knew I was going to be at each of those places because He sent me there. He didn't send me to die but to live, and those two experiences helped shape me into who I am today.

God knows everything about you. He knows you are reading these words right now, and He has a plan for your life that is unlike anyone else's. Yours is unique to you and will provide you with a testimony of what God can do—draw people unto Himself.

For those of you seeking out God or wondering if He even exists, I would like to challenge you to do something extraordinary. Take a chance on God and seek Him out. Read His Word and ask others who know God to help you know Him.

There is a God who is alive, who is the same yesterday, today, and forever and that is the God I wish to share with you. He is my all in all and what I live for, and I hope He is yours too.

One thing that people are constantly saying to me and about me is that I have a story for every situation. While I was visiting my daughter at her college, a friend of hers named Kyle said to me out of the blue, "I came up to talk to you because I wanted to hear one of your stories of what God is doing in your life."

One December a few years ago, I was walking from my truck to the back door of my grocery store after I had just told someone a story and they were deeply touched by it. Thinking about that moment I said out loud to God, "Why is it when people ask me a question pertaining to You or to life in general, do I always have a story for them?"

God said: "John, I am making you like me."

Tears began to come as I thought about those words. I have heard preachers many times say God is calling us to be Christlike, but I never quite thought of it like that.

As the years have gone by and I look back, I can see why stories are so useful. The parables Jesus told were stories His culture could easily understand. The stories God has given me also speak to the cultures I visit.

Looking Back

We often see God's handiwork in all that has been accomplished for Him. He even shows us the times when He came to our aid and guided us back onto the path He has for us. This is especially true for me on the overseas trips God has sent me on.

As I look back at Nepal, Burkina Faso, and Thailand, I see a common theme—God will supply my needs. God will go with me wherever I go. The plans He has for me are better than I could ever imagine. The list goes on and on.

What if I never said yes to God? What if I just stayed home, worked, and raised my family? Would I have the same relationship that I have now with God? The answer is clearly no. When I traveled to those places, I had to lean heavily on Him because they were unfamiliar to me. So every day I got up and asked God what to do.

I had no distractions from my life at home. At home I have technology like my cell phone, computer, iPad, or Kindle. There are people coming to me constantly to visit and to get encouragement from me. I have a business that demands much of my time. My family is another blessing that I cherish and care for, but when I leave all those things behind when God calls me to go, it creates a different picture of life.

When you get to an unfamiliar foreign land, you tend to lean on the things you think will help you. In my case that is the Lord. I start my day in prayer and end my day in prayer whenever I am abroad. In those times my prayers seem much more intense as I ask the Creator to help me while I journey ahead.

The Holy Spirit teaches me more easily in those situations because I am not looking at what to do next, but what to do now. As we traveled around Nepal, I continually saw things I ordinarily would have missed. I know it was my close relationship to the Holy Spirit in those situations that helped me.

I would like to challenge you today to lay down the everyday stuff, even for only a day, and pursue God in a place you don't usually travel to and seek His will for that day. It will change your life forever.

A friend told me that once I went on a mission trip, I would be hooked for life. I never understood what he meant until I went on my first trip to Mission, Texas, for fourteen days several years ago. It was on that trip God told me to go to Nepal. After Nepal, God has continued to call me to other places, although my heart still has a tug to all the places I have already been. I am like Paul who had a longing to go back to the people he had visited in the foreign lands. I also have those same feelings.

The people I was with in those places have all asked me if I would come back. When God is at work and we all see it, we want more. What a blessing to have people around the world that I pray for every day, whom I long to be with, and for whom I would lay my life down. It is that life changing.

As you get up tomorrow or head to your bedroom tonight, I pray that you pursue God in such a way that He will take you from your everyday life to a day where you see God at work as you never have before, and from that day forward your life will never be the same.

And now, my stories....

WHEN I AM NOT FAITHFUL

My first story is one about my writing this book. It has not come easy for me and was never on my bucket list of things to do, so when God suddenly said to write a book for Him years ago, I didn't get too excited about it. I have continually kept a journal and notes of what has been happening through the past few years, but I have not been faithful to keep on writing this book day in and day out.

After some months had passed without my writing anything, God again spoke to me and said, "Write the book I have asked you to write." I was immediately convicted and troubled about my lack of faithfulness and my disobedience to do what He asked of me even though it seemed like an unrealistic task.

God always has a way to encourage me to do what He is asking of me. Sometimes it is through others, lots of times though reading His Word, but on the day God challenged me to write this book, it was through a devotion I was reading.

The passage of the day was a short one, John 14:1, "Don't let your hearts be troubled." That passage immediately brought tears to my eyes as I thought about my situation.

In John 14, Jesus Himself was about to die and He was the One giving advice to the disciples about not letting things frighten them. He told them they needed to trust in the plan the Father had.

As I read the previous chapter, it said that one of the disciples was going to betray Jesus, and Peter was going to deny Him three times. Jesus told them that He would be with them only a little longer and then would be taken from them. It was after giving those messages to them that Jesus said, "Don't let your hearts be troubled."

Jesus was telling them to trust God and to trust Him. This was not easy because their world seemed to be collapsing around them, and they must have been deeply troubled.

The good news for us is we know the story and what happened. We understand the results of Jesus going to the cross for our sins, and we know what the disciples did after Jesus went up to heaven to be seated at the right hand of God. So it would seem easy for us to do as God asks. Unfortunately it's not so when you are placed in a position that is troubling and you do not know the outcome.

Such encouragement from Jesus—looking back would be just what they *needed* but not what they *wanted*. They wanted Him to stay. They didn't want things to change and now He was encouraging them with, "It will be okay."

I know my Creator, who loves me and has called me His own, has given me a task that only He can do—to use me to write a book. I am a grocer from South Dakota, with no training in this area, and yet God said, "Write a book for Me."

When I look back, it is so easy to see that God has been faithful; and in the times when I was not faithful, He was so patient with me and has shown me such mercy. He gives grace and taught me when I am not faithful. His promises remain true.

This book is here today not because of me, but because

God is faithful to complete what He has set out to do and that was to get me to write a book for Him.

Enter his gates with thanksgiving and his courts with praise; give thanks to him and praise his name. For the LORD is good and his love endures forever, his faithfulness continues through all generations (Psalm 100:4-5).

Callie

My cat's name is Callie and she has been given a task to do and has done it well. Some or even most would discount what I am about to say, but it is what it is. About a month ago I went to bed weeping to the Lord and apologizing that I had not been faithful to Him about writing this book that He had asked me to write. After asking God to help me find some time to write, I was off to sleep for the night.

The next morning I felt my cat sitting on my chest, and as I opened my eyes I saw the clock read 4:55 am. In my house it would actually be 4:35 am, since I set my clock twenty minutes fast, to be on time for work. So for your sake I will use the time I saw, which was 4:55 am.

I was pretty groggy. I petted my cat and then said to her, "Callie, you need to go back to sleep." She meowed even more for me to get up. This had never happened before, and she is over fifteen years old. I got up and placed some food out for her and went back to bed.

I fell asleep and about 7 am I was awakened by a paw that was gently tapping on my face. And again the cat was sitting on my chest and was attempting to wake me up. I got up and let her outside and got dressed and ready for work.

All day I thought about what had happened. It was completely odd that the cat would wake me. I could not help but wonder why the change in her habits. She usually sleeps through my getting up and going to work and rarely gets up early for anything.

Well, the next morning I felt a tap on my face and again I awoke and looked up and saw the clock say 4:55 am. *Wow that seems weird!* I thought, but again I got up and attended to her needs or what I thought were her requests of me. (I will admit I do love my cat more than many people would.)

Since that day this has happened like clockwork every single morning. It is now a regular occurrence to wake at 4:55 am. Somewhere during this time I came to figure out the cat was doing the will of God. Yes, the will of God. This may seem strange and it is, but I believe that God is using my cat to prepare me for writing every morning by starting my day when the clock reads 4:55 am.

So today as you read this, it was my first time at writing at this time of the day. Thank you, Lord, for finding me time to write this book. It has been a journey and will continue to be one because finding time to write has been a tough task for me to do.

Thank You for Your plans for my life and for the life of the reader of this book. Your plans are always best and Your thoughts are always right. Sorry it took a month of wake up calls to get the message You were bringing to me. Thank You, Lord, for You are good.

PICKLED PIGS' FEET

As a fifth grader, I remember my first experience with a family who was truly poor. A boy whom I had befriended in school was longing for someone to show kindness to him, and as a naïve boy who loved everyone, I had no idea what that meant to him.

Our relationship only lasted a year before his family moved from town, but it was a year I will never forget. What I saw was a family knit together with love for each other, a family who had to prepare and sacrifice to get to do most anything. The lesson learned was an important lesson in my life.

Playing after school at his house was always fun, and with no toys that I ever saw, we made up our own games and ways to have fun. We played outdoors mostly, and even when the weather seemed poor, it didn't hamper our enthusiasm for creating an environment for those special days.

As time went along, I went to a drive-in movie theater and told them how exciting the movie was and that made the kids want to experience it too. So after a week or so passed, I was invited to go with them to the outdoor movie theater.

I remember going two times with them. The first was their first time going there, and I had the privilege of showing them where to park, how to hook up the speaker, and where the concession stand was.

The concession stand cost money, and I didn't realize they didn't have money for it. I asked when we were going in to get our popcorn and pop, and I could see the look on their faces that I had made a big mistake. Their mom let me know they brought their food so they wouldn't miss any of the movie by going into the stand for food.

The movie hadn't started yet, and she told me I could go in if I liked. Not feeling that would be proper, I said no that I would have what they had. Their mom and dad smiled as they took out a gallon jar of pickled pigs' feet, handed out napkins, and one pig's foot per person. As they came around to me, I couldn't do it. In my mind it was something not to be eaten, but in theirs it was a treat.

I could see the disappointment in their mom's face. First that I didn't take one and second that I would be sitting without anything to eat after she knew I had intentions of going to the food stand earlier. Nothing much was said after that about the food or anything else. It was glossed over, and I was dropped off at home with a thank you for going with them and a thank you for taking me exchanged as we parted that evening.

After the movie I thought about this for a long while, and at my family's grocery store I spoke with our butcher Ralph about the pigs' feet, and I will never forget what he said. He said: "John, if you were truly his friend, you would have eaten that pig's foot and smiled."

I said I couldn't do it, and as we sat there in the backroom of the store, Ralph left and came back with a jar of pigs' feet. He opened it up, bit into one, and handed me another one. I said no again, but after some coaxing I took one out of the jar. I can't say I liked it that day, but it prepared me for my next step that would come later.

The day came again when I was invited to go with them

to the drive-in and I accepted the invite. Upon arriving, the mom pulled out a big bag of popcorn she had popped at home for this special night. After the last time, she felt the need to have something I would want to have. They didn't have enough money to buy from the food stand, but she could pop popcorn.

As she handed out the popcorn, she came to me and began to give me some. I asked her where the pigs' feet were, and I could see the whole family paused. They knew it was something I didn't like so they hadn't brought them out this time.

The next set of words were not easy for me to say, but I felt were necessary, "I was hoping you brought the pigs' feet so I could have one with you."

She said: "Are you sure you want one?" Yes was my reply, and at that moment, they all had the biggest smiles on their faces. They would now get to have what they really wanted without feeling bad about having a guest who didn't like them.

They got them out of the trunk of the car and handed me one and I ate the pig's foot, yes all of it to the bone. I ate it smiling, knowing the freedom it gave to this great family. To enjoy what they loved that day was like giving them the greatest present I could have given.

I found out you can and should do most anything for a friend, if you truly love them. Giving up your wants for a friend is one of the greatest gifts you can offer, and it doesn't take money, wealth, or anything of material value to show you love them.

The greatest value you have is what you have done for others and the relationships you develop in this life. The other things will all fade away. Your home, car, computer, books, and the like will all mean nothing when you pass from this earth.

It is those lives you touched that will count at the end of your life. Don't waste another day; invest your time in someone you love and let them know you care. The lesson I learned that day has allowed me to travel the world and eat everything set before me and be able to be a blessing everywhere I go.

Bernie and Richard

As a teen, for whatever reason, I seemed to take notice of those less fortunate than I was and often took action to help them out as best I could. I remember coming in contact with two brothers, Bernie and Richard, who were probably both under ten years old the first time we met, and how I felt the urge to be a part of their lives.

They lived in a trailer across from our grocery store and had no dad living with them. I saw a need and thought I could invest in their lives for the better of both them and me. So I pursued a friendship with them.

My relationship with them was built on a need I saw they had for someone to encourage them and give them a sense of value that they didn't seem to have in their lives. So our journey began and would not really pause until they moved away years later.

They had a past of stealing things, mostly as a way to get something they couldn't see they could ever get otherwise. They also had a passion for finding and seeking out new things. This didn't always mix well, and that is where I saw an opportunity to help.

I remember taking them to places where they had never been before—on a fishing trip, to a movie theatre, a fireworks stand, restaurants, and an ice cream shop.

People questioned why I would be associating with these two boys and why I would even care about them or their needs. I didn't care what people felt about it because what I was doing was getting to see them experience things for the first time in their lives with such anticipation and enthusiasm that the excitement rubbed off on me also. Nothing like that in my life ever touched me as much as serving them until years later when my wife and I started our own family.

Giving of your time means the world to those who don't know anyone who seems to care about them. Those two grew up knowing I cared, and yes I did care. As the years passed and they moved, it would be almost 15 years until I saw Bernie again. As I was walking through a mall one day, Bernie and I spotted each other. Richard, I learned that day, had died in a car accident a few months earlier.

I told Bernie how sorry I was at the loss of Richard, and as we talked, Bernie shared how our experiences together helped shape their lives and also how often he and Richard spoke of me and what I meant to them both through the years. Tears began to stream down my face as he spoke of his life since our days together.

Bernie went on to have a family and was there for them. He shared the reason he was investing so much in their lives was because he was shown love at a time when love came none too often. We shared our family pictures and he showed me the tattoo he had done himself and also thanked me for taking the time years earlier to be his friend.

As my wife, Jill, came out of a store, she saw me hugging

Bernie in the middle of the mall, a man whom she had never seen before. She walked over to us and after being introduced, Bernie shared what our relationship meant to him and his brother.

As we finished up our conversation, we hugged, exchanged phone numbers, and said our goodbyes. After we parted, my wife took my hand and said, "Thank you for being a part of their lives" and that she knew I was going to be a great dad, in part because of those experiences.

Serving others is never a waste of time. It is an investment in others that you may or may not ever get the privilege to see bear much fruit, but it is an investment you need to make.

Every man shall give as he is able, according to the blessing of the LORD your God which He has given you (Deuteronomy 16:17).

OWNERS OF A GROCERY

After living two years in Moose Lake, Minnesota, Jill and I moved to Gettysburg, South Dakota. We were given the chance to come back home to South Dakota and start a new life and be owners of our first business, a grocery store.

As we prepared to move, we had to have our trailer house hauled to its new location. We sought out a mover and found one from Winner, South Dakota, my childhood hometown. The movers came up to Moose Lake, hooked on our trailer, and off we went.

We had a truck, a car, and their tractor trailer that was pulling our entire home and all its contents. As we traveled down the road, we seemed to be having no problems until suddenly we ran into a rainstorm, which wasn't too bad. Still things seemed to go well, but as we approached St. Cloud, Minnesota, our tire blew and an axel bent. We would have to stay two days in a hotel until it could be fixed.

The next day, as we sat in our room with the drivers enjoying a football game and a few drinks, one of the drivers saw the words John 3:16 on a fan's poster at the game and asked what that was about. I shared the verse from heart, "For God so loved the world that he gave his one and only son, that whoever believes in him shall not perish, but have eternal life."

Upon hearing this, one driver wanted to know more about that verse, while the other made some comments about not wishing to hear that garbage. I left it at that, knowing the one didn't want us to ruin his night of drinking. As we sat there, I began to ponder how I would find an opportunity to share about who this Jesus was and is. I began to pray for the right opportunity to share the good news and then waited.

We began to head out the following day and all seemed to go well again until we got near Milbank, South Dakota, when the tongue of the trailer collapsed. We would again have to spend a night in a motel. This time my wife and the driver who showed no interest in God went on to our destination while the other driver and I decided to finish the move by ourselves.

This gave me an opportunity I had prayed for, and as luck would have it, John 3:16 was again waved from the stands that night as we began watching another football game.

I asked if he wanted to finish our conversation we started the night before. He said yes and as we talked, he came to a point where he said he wished to know this Jesus in a personal way, just as he had heard. So we prayed and he accepted Christ as his personal Savior and Lord.

After we finished talking that night and went on to Gettysburg, our relationship didn't completely end there. I was in contact with him on and off, through letters and phone calls mostly, and one visit from each of us. He got active in a church and began living for Christ and became a leader in his church. John 3:16 had changed this man's life, and God gave me the privilege to come along for the ride. It really wasn't luck that John 3:16 was on the screen; God knew it would be there and used it for His glory.

If we are open to His leading, God will use us for great things. I have said many times in my life the greatest thing we can accomplish in life, besides accepting the Lord ourselves, is to lead someone to the Lord and watch that person grow closer to Him.

Success

When my college years had ended, I decided to set up a few goals and they were as follows: Number one, "I want to become manager of a grocery store by the time I am 25." Number two, "I want to own a grocery store by the time I am 30." Number three, "I want to own two businesses by the time I am 35." I accomplished all of them by the time I was 23.

I was a success in the eyes of the world with my own grocery store, but my life was falling apart. My marriage was strained by my long hours of work. My drinking was turning into a dependence on alcohol, and I had other bad habits taking over my life. I was approaching the end of my life as I knew it, and something was about to explode if I couldn't get things under control.

At 2:30 one morning as I lay in bed, I came to the end of my rope. I cried out to God, "Lord, I need you to be Lord of my life." I realized I had accepted Jesus as my Savior, but I had failed to give my life over to Him.

As the tears streamed down my face, I decided life could not go on if things didn't change. I cried out to God, saying my life had no value to me, so "If you want it, God, I will give it to You to do with as You wish," and He responded to my prayer.

As I reached out to God that night, something special happened. I was sitting up in bed in the corner of the room when suddenly the brightest light you could ever imagine appeared and lit up my room. The room was so illuminated that

I could see my wife peacefully sleeping. I pinched myself to make sure I was awake and then the light went right through me and complete calmness came over me—a peaceful feeling that I describe as something only God could give. In that moment I knew God took the burdens of alcohol and the other addictions from my life. God was my deliverer!

A simple grocer with little to offer was given deliverance by the Creator of all things. It was so incredible that the next two years of my life would be filled with nothing but Jesus. Every hour of every day was consumed with thoughts of Him who saved me. I grew faster spiritually than at any time before or since those precious years.

I do not know why it took this miracle for me to believe, but it changed my life from that day on forever. I could not go back to my old self, for the new had come and the old had gone.

After that night I never drank again and when temptation came years later, my favorite verse came to mind.

No temptation has seized you except what is common to man. And God is faithful; he will not let you be tempted beyond what you can bear. But when you are tempted, he will also provide a way out so that you can stand up under it (1 Corinthians 10:13).

What God is saying in that verse is that He understands what we are going through. He will be there for us and when we have a temptation come our way, He will help us say no to it, help us run from it, and help us stay away from it. He is our deliverer.

THE BED

After my oldest son was ready for his first bed, my wife and I began to look at want ads for a twin bed for him. We thought a guest bed would be nice, so we began to look for larger used beds. Being a young married couple meant we had little money for new furniture.

One day I found the perfect bed and it came with some extras. It was going to be offered in an auction a few blocks from my house on my day off work. I wouldn't need to take time off to go and bid, and I had a pickup to haul it home.

As I stood at the auction that day to bid, I saw a friend who had just been through a bitter divorce and gotten custody of his son, but his daughter had stayed with his ex-wife. He had both kids on most weekends but missed his family very much the way it once was.

As we spoke I noticed he wasn't bidding on anything, and since the bed hadn't come up for auction yet, we continued to talk. He mentioned how he had spent the last six months in his apartment with his son. He had given him his bed to sleep on and shared how he had been sleeping on the floor so he was at the auction to bid on the bed.

All I could think of was that I didn't need the bed that badly, so when the bidding began on the bed, I remained quiet. The bed went for less than one hundred dollars, which was about four hundred dollars less than I was willing to spend until I heard his story.

After the auction was over, he told me he didn't have a

way to get it home, so we lifted it into my truck and hauled it to his house. On the way he said, "Hey, you didn't bid on anything. What happened that kept you from bidding? Was it the price?" I told him I didn't need it that badly, not mentioning the item was the bed he had just bought.

The thrill of seeing him have a great bed at a low price so that he could stop sleeping on the floor made my day. When I got home, my wife asked if I hauled the bed home. I laughed and said I got to haul the bed to someone else's home.

I explained it to her and we laughed at how the day went. We did get another bed, but passing the opportunity to get that bed was a great learning experience for me. It taught me in life sometimes giving up things we think we must have will give us the opportunities to help others have what they really do need.

THE DOORKNOB

After God freed me from alcohol, I pursued Him with all my heart to know Him better. This went on for two years of intense spiritual growth, but I didn't see much fruit during that time. My wife would say there was much fruit, but I wasn't seeing it.

I ended one day that was like any other—nothing special, like most days. Feeling this way I went to prayer to ask God to use me for His purpose. I laid it all out to Him—I was wishing to be a part of His plan, and it was my heart's desire to be used by Him. After pleading with Him to use me, I drifted off to sleep; but I will never forget what happened the next day.

I woke up, forgetting what I had prayed the night before and headed off to work. From the time the back door closed as I left for work until the end of the day when I sat in my bedroom to talk to God, my day was filled with Him.

I can't recall all the events of that day, but I can remember praying for someone with cancer in the backroom of my store and being called to go to the hospital to visit someone hurting. I remember seeing God at work throughout the day. When the end of my workday came, my mom called me into the office and told me that there was someone who needed to talk to us so we waited for her to come.

Upon her arrival, my mom and I heard how she was thinking of killing herself and how she felt her life was not worth living. Our hearts sank but we shared with her about the life God would give her if she just gave herself to Him. It could be a life filled with God, a Friend who would be there for her through thick and thin, never giving up on her, no matter what came before her. When she said she wanted that peace in her life, we prayed with her and saw a new life open up before our eyes.

The rest of my day was filled with most of the same fantastic experiences, and God allowed me to see how He could answer a prayer so quickly and precisely that it would build my faith up to a new level for years to come.

As the day came to an end and I once again sat in my bedroom to talk to God, I was awestruck and speechless before Him. Not only had He answered my prayer, but never before had an answer been that visible to me. I had what would be my first real two-way conversation with God.

Remembering that His Word says in heaven there are many rooms and that Jesus is building a place for those who believe, I began to talk to God, thanking Him for the day.

I gave Him one request. I believe that God and I had a good laugh together when I said, "Since I know we have rewards in heaven for things we do on earth for You, I would like to put in a request." After a pause, I asked for a doorknob for my house in heaven. It may seem crazy, but as I thought about what had transpired during the day, I came to a place where I acknowledged that my part in it was next to nothing. I knew I had actually very little to do with the outcome of it all.

Yes, God had used me, but it was He who changed hearts and gave comforting words to those who needed it that day through me. And as great as it was, my part deserved less than a doorknob.

I don't know if God is giving me a cool doorknob, no doorknob, or if He is calling me a doorknob, but I do know that when He decides to use us, He can, and that it will be better than anything we could ever imagine. Our God is not confined to our simple mind. God can do great things through those who love Him.

I am the vine; you are the branches. If you remain in me and I in you, you will bear much fruit; apart from me you can do nothing (John 15:5).

TRAINING

Train up a child in the way he should go, And even when he is old he will not depart from it (Proverbs 22:6).

He called a little child to him, and placed the child among them. And he said: "Truly I tell you, unless you change and become like little children, you will never enter the kingdom of heaven. Therefore, whoever takes the lowly position of this child is the greatest in the kingdom of heaven (Matthew 18:2-4).

These verses speak of how we are to raise our children and how we are to become like little children, trusting God in all we do, and living for Him.

A pastor once shared a story of how God trained him for a purpose. The pastor was in bed one night and he heard God tell him to crawl out of bed and lay on the floor. He didn't do it at first, questioning what he heard and wondering if it were truly God's voice.

Again God told him to get out of bed and lay on the floor. This time he knew it was God and crawled out of his warm bed in the middle of winter and lay down on the cold floor. After he followed God's instructions, He told my friend to go back to bed.

How strange, he thought and then the next night it happened again. This time he started questioning God about it but received no answer.

This went on for months, and after a while it was just a

normal part of his night. God told him to move and he moved right to the floor. He quit questioning God and just did it with a childlike faith that God knew what He was doing.

Then one day in the summer the pastor was driving home when he came upon a bridge with many people standing outside their cars looking at an object. After getting out of his car and approaching the crowd, he saw their attention was fixed on a woman who was about to jump to her death from the bridge.

The pastor thought maybe he could talk her down and so he walked over to her. When he was within several feet of the woman, she jumped over the rail and off the bridge.

Immediately the pastor heard God say, "Save her!" and he jumped over the rail to the water below and was able to save the woman. Later, upon reflecting on all that happened, he began to see why he had been trained to lay on the floor when God asked.

You see, if God wouldn't have trained him to react so quickly to His voice, she would have died. With the strong current and distance to the river, it would have been all over quickly if he hadn't responded immediately. Without looking over the rail and thinking that this might be a bad outcome for him if he jumped, he went ahead and followed God's word. The pastor said he might have just looked on like the rest of the crowd, and she would have been gone. Instead, God used that winter to train him to obey His voice.

What a wonderful story of how God had a plan to save a woman months before she tried to end her life, and how God wanted to show a pastor how to trust Him better! In the end God's plans are always to be trusted.

If we think about small children, we see how they trust us to help them as they grow. The mistrust comes later, after they experience life and see all is not the way it should be in this world.

Children do not question your love for them; they do not question that your plan is good. They just accept it as truth and move on with it.

If only we would do that all the time. If we could hear from God and just do as He asks, knowing that it is best for us, even if we don't see over the rail on the bridge or the view we see is one where there seems to be no hope and that all will be lost. No matter what we see, God's plan is best for us, no matter the cost.

But with God all things are possible. Romans 8:28 says,

And we know that in all things God works for the good of those who love him, who have been called according to his purpose.

ALL MY MONEY, LORD

During the first two years after giving my life to God, I grew spiritually leaps and bounds and then some challenges arose. God seemed to be grooming me for something bigger than anything I could have ever imagined, and it began with my next step of faith.

As usual I was sitting in my bedroom talking to God and reading His Word. When I pondered what He would have for me to do, I was given a task that would help shape my giving habits for all the rest of my days.

I felt God telling me something, but I thought I was hearing wrong. I felt Him tell me to give all my money away. Between what I was reading and what I heard Him tell me, I knew what I was supposed to do—drain everything from our bank accounts and give it all away.

The next few moments I contemplated what was about to happen. First, where would the money come from to pay all our bills? We had a new home; a vehicle payment; gas, electricity, and garbage bills; and our tithe to the church. How would we make it through the month without money? I began to move toward the door to talk to my wife, Jill.

As I approached her, she could see that something was on my mind. Looking at my face, she asked what was going on, and I searched for just the right words. All I could say was that God wanted us to give away all our money. She asked, "All of it?" and I replied, "Yes, all of it." I will never forget her reaction to my statement. She said if God said do it then go ahead and do it. Wow, she had more faith than I had or she didn't understand fully what I had said because I do all the bills each month.

The next day I went to the bank and removed everything we had in our checking and savings accounts and also emptied my wallet and placed all the money in an envelope. I headed directly to the home where God told me to go. As the door opened and I handed the wife the envelope, I wondered what God was giving it to that family for. I told the woman that God instructed me to give it to them. The reaction I got back from the woman was not very helpful to me in understanding why God would have this plan for me.

She took it, said thanks, and shut the door quickly, leaving me standing there speechless. I remember saying to myself, "Well, that was not what I was expecting." To this day I do not know what they needed the money for. That was not for me to know; I just needed to give them the money and walk away.

The following day something incredible happened to me. Someone came up and said they felt they should give me a check. I saw that the total on it was within $2 of the amount we had just given away the day before!

I got to see God at work for the cost of a mere $2. In the end He didn't take it all; He just borrowed it for a day and gave it back. I believe He asked me to do that as a way of allowing me to see how far I was willing to go for Him as a response to the One who gave up everything for me (Jesus).

He knew I would do it for Him, but I didn't know until I went through with His plan. After that day I had more faith to do His will more easily. I was able to see the results of His faithfulness when I gave away all that I had for Him, and that lesson has continued to teach me from that day forward.

PROMISE KEEPERS

The first year Promise Keepers was held in the mile high stadium in Denver was the first year I attended. I am not going to take time to explain the movement but only give you some idea of how it changed my life.

After attending Promise Keepers that year, three men from my church decided to work on getting fifty men from our community to go the next year. We met often for prayer and to look for ways to encourage other men to go. We also set out to find a way we could travel together to share the experience with each other.

In the end we traveled on three full buses to Denver with two other communities, and later that same year, another group from our church went to Promise Keepers in Minneapolis. The point is that I enjoyed it so much that I encouraged others to go.

Promise Keepers taught me to be a servant leader to my wife and family. They taught me to clean up my act so that my family could see a better me and hopefully a Christ-like example to follow. The commitment to Promise Keepers helped me stay on track with the Lord, my family, and my church.

I heard a story at one of the meetings of a man who was friends with two men for his entire adult life. He never saw them come to know the same Lord he loved in his lifetime, but at his funeral one gave his life to the Lord. The other friend did so a couple years later. He died not knowing the impact he had on their lives and that the life he led would eventually be a huge factor that would move them to want to know God personally like he did.

They also spoke one year of a man who wanted to see three hundred men from his community come to an event. He was diagnosed with cancer that year and never made it to the next year's event. What he didn't know was that three hundred men came to fulfill his dream. The ironic thing about that was his son-in-law came and gave his heart to Jesus at the event that year. Another incredible story of how God can use a life for His glory.

At one event I attended, they asked for one million men to commit to going to Washington DC to pray for one day in October 1997 to ask God to heal our land. That year I knew it would be tough on us financially for me to go, so I asked God to make a way for me.

I saved ten dollars a week until the event the next year. When the time neared, some men from Pierre, South Dakota, invited me to go with them on a plane they booked to DC. The price was a little less than the five hundred I had saved up for the trip and included a bus ride and subway tickets to the event and great fellowship with new friends. I was the only one from my town to go, and I felt it was a privilege.

Going to the Mall in Washington DC gave me some of the most incredible experiences. We were also asking Him to give us clean hearts and a new start, while helping us reach out and tell others the good news of Jesus. Seeing over one million men bowing to the Creator of the world and asking Him to save us from the path our country was heading on touched me deeply.

I have taken all four of my children to Promise Keepers events and that includes my daughter. Promise Keepers strengthened my marriage, my relationship with God, and my commitment to my local church and the body of Christ.

It was a time when I needed to see other men with struggles too come and listen to the different speakers explain God's Word. We could see that Jesus gave us the perfect example of how to live our lives with purpose and how to leave a legacy that would last for generations to come.

My hope for you too is to live a life that will reflect God onto your children and grandchildren for generations to come. If you do not have a wife or children, you still have people watching your life.

Leave a legacy of a lifetime commitment to God to those who so desperately need to see what it is like to be sold out and fully devoted to the Lord.

FALLING APART

In 1998 my life seemed to be going along just fine. I had a great relationship with God that kept me close to Him and far from my past life. He had changed me full circle into a man of God, but life was about to change, and at that time, not for the better. It was going to be a time of testing for me and a time to gain a new growing dependence on God.

A series of health crises were coming upon us. My wife, Jill, would have her neck fused in two places, and both our youngest children would develop serious health issues.

One day Joshua stopped breathing for about three minutes, but finally began to breathe on his own. For the next two years we would have to monitor him for any colds, fever, flu, or a sudden spike in temperature. If he looked sick, he was taken to the hospital. He could not get a rapid rise in fever, or he could stop breathing and not start up again. Jacob had a virus so severe that he was hospitalized for two days with what was thought to be a burst appendix.

During this time I had rotator cuff surgery, and after a couple weeks, tore my bicep and had to have it reattached to my arm. My life was falling apart, and at the time it looked like a horrible ride that never ends. All this happened in a short time period, and my world came crashing down. I don't know how we got through it, but I can tell you that my pastor mowed our lawn, and the wives of men from my Bible study cooked meals for us. My church family offered whatever was needed, and I will be forever be grateful.

God granted me triumph in the midst of testing, joy in the midst of sorrow, and peace in the midst of trouble. I wouldn't wish to have this happen again, and I do not take good health for granted, yet God made me a better man through it. I became sensitive to those in the hospital and in nursing homes, and those with health issues. Now I am more likely to be one of the first ones to call or visit someone in need.

The troubles that came to my family forced me to recognize God's importance in my life and the people He places in our lives. It also helped me to recognize people in need who need a prayer, a visit, a card, a hand to hold onto, or just someone with whom they can have a good cry.

Remember there are those who are hurting and in need of your words of encouragement, probably even as you are reading this book. Take time today to touch someone who is hurting. Show people the love they need in a time of trouble, and you will also be blessed.

Praise be to the God and Father of our Lord Jesus Christ, the Father of compassion and the God of all comfort, who comforts us in all our troubles, so that we can comfort those in any trouble with the comfort we ourselves receive from God (2 Corinthians 1: 3-4).

THE MAN FROM TURKEY

As a Rotarian, I have had the privilege to meet many people who wish to serve others. The Rotarians motto is: "Service above self." One week several years ago, I was asked to help a group of Rotarians from Turkey comprised of one man and several women.

They were on an exchange program to visit our area of the world to get an overall view of life in South Dakota. My job was to drive them from place to place so they could see what we had to offer. I said yes, so they came to Gettysburg, and off we went to sightsee.

As we drove from place to place, the man saw my One Year Bible in between the seats of my van and asked if I was a follower of Jesus. "Yes I am" was my answer, and with some encouraging words I found out he was curious about what makes Christianity different from other religions.

Ironically I had been studying other faiths the previous few months to get a grasp of their beliefs, so I had the knowledge to tackle some of his tough questions. We were together for a couple days, and we had plenty of time between stops and dinners and the like to get to visit quite a bit.

The day he was to leave, he said to me that he wished he had a Bible to read. The problem was it needed to be in his language, for he didn't read English very well. Finding a Turkish Bible in our country is next to impossible, so I guessed it probably wouldn't happen.

Then it hit me. I had been to Promise Keepers the past

year and received ten Bibles to mail to Turkey. I had mailed them, but one of them had been returned from Turkey because it was religious material and the family who received it didn't wish to have it. So instead of simply throwing it away, they refused it and it was sent back to me.

I went home and dug through my boxes with Bibles and found it. I hurried back and handed him that Bible and asked if it was in his language. He smiled and said yes. He said he would take it back to Turkey and read it.

We both stood in amazement that a grocer from South Dakota would have a Bible for a man from Turkey, but looking back it was how God intended it to happen. There was no doubt that God showed His love for this man and had a Bible for him when the man reached the point of asking for one.

Think about how God cares for us. He feeds the birds of the earth and they don't worry about food. How much more do you think God loves us? When that man called out to God because he reached a point in his life when he wanted to hear about Jesus, God already had in place the Bible that was needed. This man asked and God responded right there and provided him with a Bible.

It was not just by chance I went to Promise Keepers, received ten Bibles, mailed them to Turkey, and one came back. It was not by chance that I had a Bible for this man when he needed it. It was God's perfect timing and God's chance to reveal Himself to this man.

CHURCH SERMONS

As the years have passed, I became aware my church had only one person who was willing to do the message on Sundays when our pastor was out of town or unable to be there. Our church had over 100 people each week, but no one else from our church filled the pulpit.

Maybe they weren't asked; maybe they said no; whatever the reason, there seemed to be a problem. As a new deacon to the board, I saw how Myron had to fill in. He made the comment that with the failing health of our current pastor, he needed to keep a sermon in his back pocket because he had been asked with short notice to do some Sunday sermons.

I decided to take it to God and ask Him why there wasn't anyone else willing to step up. What happened was not what I wanted to hear. I laid it out to him how Myron was our main source in the church to fill the pulpit and the strain it put on him.

About a minute into the conversation, God turned it back to me and said, "What about you?" "No way," I said, and again He took the conversation back to me. I thought about it and said, "First, I have never done anything like that before; and second, there must be someone else You can ask." I even gave Him my list of people to ask.

God was having nothing to do with my suggestions because He was working on me and my stepping up and out of my comfort zone for Him. I decided I would tell our pastor that I would be available if he felt he needed me to fill the pulpit, so I headed out the door of my house to see him.

When I got to his house he wasn't there, but his wife was and she said he was mowing someone's yard on Hilltop Drive. I headed up there and when I didn't see him, I felt a relief and began to drive away. I looked toward another house and could see Pastor Jim waving at me to let me know he was headed my way.

When he arrived I reluctantly let him know I was available to fill the pulpit if he ever felt he had no other options. I didn't tell him God sent me because I thought he might say yes. Well, to my surprise, he smiled and said he would put me down to fill in at the next opportunity.

That was not what I was wanting to hear, but Pastor Jim saw the need also and the opportunity it would be for me to step up in faith to serve the Lord in a way I would never have imagined.

If you were there for my first sermons, you probably would have seen I never looked up from my papers and Bible for fear I might see someone and forget what I was attempting to say. But as the years went by, I may not be totally without fear at being up front speaking about the Lord, but He has taught me it is all about Him and for His glory. If I remember that, it seems to almost always go well.

That step of faith has caused me to grow as much as anything else in my life. When you step into the pulpit to tell of what God would have for them and teach others about the God you love, you need to do your homework so that He can use you in a way that is pleasing to Him. Pray, read His Word, fast, cry out to Him, and do whatever it takes to prepare for the day you fill in for the pastor.

If you are a person who is petrified of being up front, I

understand because I was one of those people. If you give God the chance to help you when you are asked to do something for Him, you will have no greater joy. I can't say I enjoyed those first few sermons, but they helped make me the man of God I am today. Without stepping out in faith, you will not grow.

You need to take a chance and let God work through you. So the next time you are asked to do the impossible, ask God to help you and let your light shine for Jesus. With God all things are possible. He shines brighter in times when people who seem unusable are used.

SEEING IS BELIEVING

Many years ago I received a gift on Father's day from Jacob. My son didn't give me a tie or something he bought but something better. He took the time to make a picture for me. As I glanced down at it, I saw a man standing next to a much smaller child. This was Jake and I standing beside each other.

Upon examining it closer, I noticed something on the shirt he had me wearing. It simply said on the shirt, "I Love God." I didn't own a shirt like that, but Jacob knew the most important thing in my life was and is God. He had seen me serve others through the years, become a deacon, and even preach God's Word some Sunday mornings.

Even though you would not expect small children to be examining our lives, they are watching our every move. They see us struggle and they see us succeed; and what I noticed as I grow older is you cannot change or alter someone's view of you with simple words. If they see us doing something wrong we can't say, "Do as I say, not as I do."

It is from our actions that we are judged, and people will decide what they think makes us click. Even when we are doing what is wrong and think that it is a secret only we know, you would be surprised how your loved ones would say to you that they knew it all along.

As you go through life, remember there are people watching you and some of them are the little children who come into our lives and are looking for someone to look up to. Be that person who is living the life God wishes for them to live. Live a life that is pleasing to the Lord in private, not just in view of all. I try and live my life realizing that someone could be watching me at any time and also knowing God is watching me all the time.

Jacob made me more aware that I need to be on guard for his sake (and also mine) of the things that would harm my relationship with God and also distort his view of God. We are to be a living example of how to live as Jesus lived.

Therefore, I urge you, brothers and sisters, in view of God's mercy, to offer your bodies as a living sacrifice, holy and pleasing to God—this is your true and proper worship (Romans 12:1).

VIEW FROM A DAUGHTER

In the seventh grade, my daughter Justine was asked to write something about her parents. My wife saw the papers and made copies of them for me to see. Jill handed me a copy with a great big smile on her face and told me to read them.

The first story Justine wrote was about her mom. She wrote: "My hero is my mom. She is my hero because of all she does for me. My mom is someone I can look up to for advice. She has been through a lot and she can help me a lot and always has her opinions on things.

"She is also funny and has a good personality. My mom is the kind of person that everyone enjoys being around. She is the funniest person I will ever know; even in hard situations she can ease tension."

After reading this about my wife, I turned to my page and began to read what Justine wrote about me. "The parent that I exhibit my best qualities to is my dad. I don't get to see him all the time because he is always working, but when I do talk to him, he seems to always challenge me. I think that I click more with my mom, but my dad does bring out my better qualities."

At this point I stopped and said to Jill, "Why am I reading this? She says she isn't as close to me and that you are her hero, and that she clicks more with you. All I see is that I am always busy and that I challenge her constantly."

Jill said, "You need to keep reading this, John." I picked up the paper, already thinking of ways to be a better father and ready to give more time to Justine, since she mentioned my lack of time for her. Here is the next part of the paper: "He always wants me to strive for more. He doesn't push me unless he knows I can do better. Sometimes I feel he is never satisfied no matter what I do, but I know that it is out of love and makes me a better person in the long run. It makes me go after what I really want and to always know that I can do better."

At that point in reading what she wrote, I still wasn't feeling the best since it seemed like I pushed her too much, but I continued on reading and an amazing thing was revealed to me in her next sentence.

Justine wrote: "I want to be like my dad when I get older. He is an amazing person. I want the love that he has for his family and for God. My dad is always amazing at whatever he does. He is definitely a person that a lot of people look up to and I want that someday, and hope to be that kind of person."

I dropped my head and tears began to go down my face. She saw all the challenges I gave her as something she needed, and she understood why I pushed her to do better.

This is at times how God works in our lives. Sometimes He allows trials to come to change our direction towards Him, to mold us to be more like Him, or even to show us how the hurts we are going through will prepare us for helping other people later.

When that day began winding down, I went straight to the Lord and asked Him to make me a better husband, father, and friend because I realized the choices I make do matter.

JUSTINE GOES TO AFRICA

I hope this next story will inspire you to listen to God and do as He wishes regardless if it makes sense or not. It is about Justine and a choice that God asked me to make. Several years ago she walked into our home one day and said, "Dad, God is sending me and Mallea (Justine's friend) to Africa." She waited for my answer.

As shocked as I was about that statement, I still managed to say: "Okay, if this is what God wants from you, then it will happen. Can I have some information about this trip and things like how much will it cost?"

She said it would cost at least $3000 each. She paused and then I asked: "When do you need it by?" She said by next week. I told her, "I guess you are gonna get your answer rather quickly then if you will go or not."

The following Sunday it was announced at our church service and by the end of the day, the offering was enough to show that it looked like the two girls were going to Africa, but there was more that needed to be done.

Two and a half weeks were left for them to get shots, plane tickets, practice music for a part of their ministry there, pray for the trip, and get passports and visas approved. How would this even be possible when I had waited over a month to get mine for a trip to Mexico earlier, and they had a little more than two weeks?

Well, it all happened, with their passport and visas arriving Friday, three days before they left for Africa. All seemed to be going perfect until Sunday night.

As I was going about my daily devotions, I was speaking to the Lord about the trip. As we conversed, God was pretty plain about what I am about to share with you. He said to me: "Get ready for a funeral."

Whoa, that is not what I wanted to hear the night before my daughter was to leave for Africa, and it was not what I expected to hear. Would I tell my wife or would I keep it to myself? Would I allow Justine to go or make her stay home?

The week before she went, I heard over and over from people how I shouldn't allow a pair of 16 year old girls go to Africa without one of their parents. Now I would send her and she could possibly not be coming back alive.

The next day I gave her the biggest hug I ever have given her and released her into God's hands. I never thought I would get to speak face to face with her again on this earth.

As the 11 day journey to Africa progressed, some not so good things happened, and this did not make me more comfortable about this whole thing, but I kept on praying. Suddenly near the end of her trip, a wonderful friend who had been struggling with cancer took a turn for the worse. Instead of months of hope to get better, she would have just a few days before going home to be with the Lord.

I got a call on my cell phone on my way home from being out of town. It was a family member asking me, on behalf of the family, to help with the funeral service. I had a long pause and said I would come over to their home in an hour when I got back in town. I pulled over to the side of the road as a flow of tears began to pour down my face. I realized then what God was trying to prepare me for but my assumptions had been that it was my daughter.

We cannot assume anything when God is giving us instructions because He knows what He wants, and we must be willing to go. I thought I was releasing my daughter to be with the Lord, but He had a different plan. In that moment I realized that I would from then on be willing to follow God's instructions to the end, even if it is on a journey I do not wish to take.

God was testing me during those days to see if I would allow His plan to progress. In the end this experience was a lot like the one Abraham faced with his son. This was my only daughter and God was asking for her, and I had to decide whether to send her away to possibly die because God was asking for her.

The following verse is what God said to Abraham just before he was about to sacrifice his son Isaac, and it explains why God would do such a thing.

"Do not lay a hand on the boy," he said. "Do not do anything to him. Now I know that you fear God, because you have not withheld from me your son, your only son" (Genesis 22:12).

It was a lesson that would not have been the same had God not told Abraham to take his son for the offering on that day. Abraham passed the test and was faithful to God, and sometime later, God would eventually send His only Son to die for us, so that we might live.

TREASURES

A few years ago I woke up from a dream and immediately I wrote down what I had seen. I knew that this was going to be a great lesson for a children's lesson at church, but that it would also be a very good lesson for those of us who are older.

When the week came for me to teach the lesson, it was planned out, prayed over, and presented on a Sunday morning at Grace Bible Church in Gettysburg, South Dakota. Here is what happened.

The children came to the front and I had a friend read some scriptures on storing up your treasures in heaven and had a time of prayer. Upon completion of that portion, I gave each child a Hershey's candy bar.

Then I had them come up on the stage and look out at the audience and said to them, "You have a candy bar and it is yours to do with as you wish. You can keep it for yourself or you can give it away to someone in the congregation, but not your parents, because you might ask them to give it back to you later."

Then after they thought about their decision, I asked them to either give it away right then or keep it. The choices were made, and they did as they wished with their candy bar.

When the time was over for acting on their decision, only one child had decided to give the candy bar away. Only one. I had planted six junior high youth to split between the two choices, so that there would be at least some on both sides of the choice. So three went with the little girl to give the candy bar away.

When they were done, I split the group up into two sides—the one that gave it and the side that kept it—and asked them to explain what that decision could mean in the future as they make other decisions like this in life.

As the little generous girl stood there, I asked her: "What do you think of this? You are the only one from your group without a candy bar and the others have one right now in their hands to enjoy."

She said, "That's okay; I wanted to give it away to someone else."

At that point the story changed as I read the verse that talks about rewards in heaven. I explained how we are to store up our treasures in heaven where moths and rust and thieves do not destroy it. I said, "Since we cannot see today what the reward would be for you for giving someone else your chocolate bar, we are going to pretend you will get to see that reward today and have it here now."

Everyone turned toward a silver case that I had a friend bring out, wondering what was inside. As he opened it, everyone could see that inside were giant Hershey's candy bars.

The little girl was excited and even thrilled to get one for herself. As I looked at the other group who had kept their candy bars, one boy in particular who had been so excited to get his treat, changed from joy to deep sadness. He saw his decision caused him not to receive the reward waiting for him.

After a brief moment to review what had just happened, one little boy asked if he could trade the small one for the big one. "No," I said, "You made your decision to keep it. Now you must have the smaller one."

The parents were deeply moved because as we looked at the scenario play out, we could see the results of the temporary pleasure we get having things here, yet it made us think of the treasures that could be waiting for us if we send them ahead by doing what God has called us all to do.

One parent later said afterwards his son sat down shaking his head and said, "I should have given it away" and was very sincere about it. Another child told me all he could do was look at the candy bar when I first brought it out and thought he just had to have it for himself. He said, "I didn't have one thought to giving it away until the treasure was revealed, and I could see what I would have gotten."

When we finished that day, I gave the big candy bars to people in the congregation and thanked them for their sacrificial giving to the Lord. One man gave his away to another who said he didn't get one.

The man who gave it away told me about it, so I gave him two more. He just smiled and showed the other man what he got in return for giving up his big candy bar.

I know we don't get to see ahead of time what God is going to give us when we die, but scripture tells us to store up our treasures in heaven for a reason. They will have great value to us. Imagine dying and having something of value given to you. You look at it and get the opportunity to lay it at Jesus' feet as a thank you to Him.

Now imagine having nothing much to give Him. At that point I am sure the treasure you could have sent ahead would be very valuable to you beyond anything you had ever imagined.

There is a place you can send treasure to that will have eternal consequences and will have a purpose when you receive them. As you begin another day here on earth, look for that opportunity to choose to send your treasures ahead of you, so that your reward will be great and your joy will be full.

Do not lay up for yourselves treasures on earth, where moth and rust destroy and where thieves break in and steal, but lay up for yourselves treasures in heaven, where neither moth nor rust destroys and where thieves do not break in and steal. For where your treasure is, there your heart will be also (Matthew 6:19-21).

THE TICKET

The South Dakota Association of Telephone Cooperatives is an association that is made up of rural telephone companies that help small towns get the telecommunication services that they need so as not to just survive but to thrive.

I have been on the State board of directors for this association, and I have been on the board of directors for one of the largest rural telephone companies for over 15 years now.

We have a state meeting each year in August, and on one particular year it was decided to have a fundraiser for Ronald McDonald house and the Special Olympics through a softball tournament.

I played in the softball game and a great time was had by all. Several thousand dollars for each charity were raised and everyone enjoyed it. That night we had our annual banquet and we heard from the two charities. As I listened to a nurse who was speaking about the Ronald McDonald House, I was deeply moved.

She told us about an elderly couple who took in a grandchild to raise and drove across the state for treatments for the child. That elderly couple stayed at the Ronald McDonald House. The nurse told us how a year after saying goodbye to that dying child, the same child walked in and gave her a hug at the house. She said, "There are still miracles being done" and that the child was healed of his terminal illness.

Tears began to stream down my face as she shared how much it encouraged her to keep serving others as a nurse and the joy she has as she gets to do what she loves doing so much each day in being a helper to those in need.

That night we had another fundraiser—a type of reverse raffle—for the charities. Half the money from ticket sales would go to that cause and the other half to the person who had the winning ticket. Each ticket would cost fifty dollars, with one hundred tickets to be sold.

The tickets were quickly sold and the drawing was about to begin. If your name was drawn, you were out of the game. You only wanted to hear your name if you were the last ticket. That would mean you won. Well, as luck would have it, Jill and I had our names drawn and we were out almost immediately.

I am not one to gamble, so I looked at it as a donation to a good cause. As the other names were drawn, it was whittled down to five names. At that point they stopped and had an auction for a ticket that would allow you to join the final group of five.

I felt a tug on my heart to buy the ticket. First, I thought *Why?* and then I said to my wife, "I think God is telling me to buy the ticket. Can I buy the ticket?" She said, "Sure, whatever you feel God is telling you to do, go ahead and do it."

As I was reaching up my hand to bid, the auctioneer cried, "Sold!" and I didn't get the ticket. At that moment I felt a bad feeling in my stomach, as I missed the opportunity I felt God was giving me. Then the auctioneer said he had the second and final ticket to sell.

I went on and bought that ticket, and at that point knew what I was supposed to do with it. As I was given the ticket, I stood up and went up to the front to the man who was running the auction and gave it to him and asked that he give it to the Ronald McDonald House representative for that charity. He made the announcement and handed it to her and she took my place with the other six people. Two more names were drawn and those tickets were eliminated. The ticket I bought was still there. The five at that point could choose to go on or they could take and divide it up equally. They chose to go on. One more name was drawn, and she was still there. Four were left.

The next name hit me hard. When they said the representative's name, she began to walk away. Suddenly one of the men stopped her and handed his ticket to her. She got to stay on the stage with the others who still had a ticket. They drew again, and again her name was drawn. Then a second man gave up his ticket for her and sat down.

Now at this point they were down to two tickets, and as they talked it over, they chose to continue to draw for one winning ticket instead of taking half for each of them.

The final name was drawn and again the representative was eliminated from the contest, and the winner was the other person. But then an incredible thing happened. The man handed his winning ticket over to her and so the Ronald McDonald House won all the money. She was deeply moved by the gesture and also said that she would like to give half the money to the Special Olympics. She had also thought of others who needed it.

It was an incredibly wonderful ending to that evening's activities. To see men give up their chance at a big pot of money to help those in need was an emotional moment for all of us watching it all play out. I could see God working from the purchase of the ticket to the end where the charities won it all. The following is a letter I got from one person who attended the meeting that night:

> The moment when you gave your reverse raffle ticket to Ronald McDonald House will stay with me for a long time. I have always told my family and friends that I love my job because of the quality and character of the people involved in the rural telecom industry. That is even more true now than ever. I just wanted you to know that I think you are a genuinely good man and I am glad that I know you.

I write this to let you who are reading this story know that people are watching our every move. One of my fellow board members handed me fifty dollars to help cover the cost of the ticket when the meeting was over. I said, "No, it was all right," but he insisted on helping and said, "Let me be a part of this special night and help you cover the cost of the ticket." I accepted his gift with gratitude and thanked him, and his look of thankfulness said it all.

We had all been a part of something bigger than ourselves that night. It was all about helping others. God did an amazing thing through the ticket, and it made us all realize the value we get from helping others.

HARVEY

The day Harvey had his stroke changed my life in ways I never expected. Sunday after Sunday he would start our church day praying for the entire church—for those coming, those leading, and those who may be thinking of coming that day.

Our church prays for everyone, every room, and for everything to be for God's glory. One particular Sunday Harvey told me he was ready to go home to heaven and that his work on earth as far as he knew was done. He was ready to see his Savior face to face. Then something unexpected happened.

Two weeks later I found myself driving to the hospital after getting the call that something had happened to Harvey. Things did not look good and as the days and weeks progressed, he would get better, but without the chance to tell us what he wished to say because Harvey had lost the ability to speak, and one side of his body could not move. He eventually would be able to squeeze my hand and smile to communicate when I visited him in the months ahead.

Sometimes you could tell he was hearing you and other times not so much. As time passed, he was placed in a home that could feed him with a tube and take care of him. The great thing about this story is that God still loves Harvey and wanted to use him for His glory. That is where our next story begins.

I was working in our meat department one Saturday by

myself because our meat man was healing from back surgery. As the morning progressed, my to-do list seemed endless when I heard God telling me to go see Harvey. I asked God if I were hearing right, and He said yes in His still quiet voice.

Upon hearing God's plan, I called Harvey's wife, Irene, and asked if it would be a problem to visit him over the lunch hour and she said no, so off I went. The trip itself was 40 miles and about halfway was a small town I drove past. At that point I remembered I hadn't asked God what He wanted me to say.

"God, what do you wish of me? What am I to say?" And in that quiet voice He said, "Tell him I love Him." The next 20 miles I pondered what was in store for Harvey and for me that day.

As I neared the room, I asked God to speak through me and that I would not be seen. He answered that prayer with an "Okay, I will." Harvey reached out his hand for me when I reached his bedside. Taking his hand I began our conversation with the fact that I had not thought of visiting him that day. I was busy and had little time to even think of going 40 miles one way to visit someone, but God remembered Harvey and wanted to reach out to him.

I told Harvey that God loved him very much and that He sent me to tell him just that. I told him I knew he didn't want to be here on earth anymore. As I spoke this, Harvey took my hand, turned it over, and began to clap using his hand slapping mine. I knew he understood what God wanted to tell him.

I told him the last friend he could still have two-way conversations with was God. Again he clapped my hand in agreement with that statement. I spoke to him about something the Bible says, and that is the prayer of a righteous man availeth much, and I knew Harvey was a righteous man. One of Harvey's strongest ministries in life is prayer and I knew it would continue to hold true.

I told him we needed his prayers for his wife, Irene, his family, his church, and those who do not know Christ yet. This was the third and final time he clapped and smiled. It was as if God had been speaking to him directly and his response through his clapping meant, "I will do as you wish, Lord, and thank You for loving me and wanting me to still be of service to You here on earth."

As the next hour and a half progressed, I spoke to him about his family and how he was so blessed to have a family who loved the Lord. As our time came to an end, we hugged and I told him I loved him and would be back sooner than later.

The trip home was a sight to see for anyone who would have seen me driving by. I was pretty much crying for 40 miles for I was blessed to have had a call from God to tell Harvey that He who made him loved him very much.

Your eyes saw my unformed body; all the days ordained for me were written in your book before one of them came to be (Psalm 139:16).

THE TRACK

When the need to talk to God arises, I head out the door to my home and often go over to the track a few blocks away or I drive out to the river 15 miles from Gettysburg. On this particular day it was the track. With the iPod on and music playing, I began to praise my Lord and Savior. It wasn't long until He began to speak to me.

At first it was me talking, as I recounted all the amazing things He had been showing me and that I had a part in. A person raised from the dead was the first one that came to mind. She was given a few days to live. She had kidney failure, cancer, and Wagner's disease. It was not good.

Then God chose to heal her as I prayed for her over the phone with her daughter, who was in Arkansas at the time. I was sitting at my desk at work in South Dakota, and the woman God healed was in Florida. She left the hospital the next day.

Then there was my foot that was healed, and recently He has put me on another journey and many people with foreign spirits have been freed from them.

As I walked, I asked God, "When will it end? When will the greater things stop happening that I am witnessing?" He said it was not going to stop but was to go on.

Then He asked me something I will never forget. "What do you wish for? Ask whatever you wish and it will be done!" I was stunned and went and sat down on a bench on the visitor's side of the field.

What would I ask? Maybe to have the lights go out in the old concession stand on the other side of the field. *No, I thought, maybe I should ask Him to have the larger stadium lights turned on,* as it was so very dark on the field that evening.

Then I looked up and saw the moon and thought maybe I will ask Him to block out the moon for a minute. As I again pondered this question, I got up and began to walk around the track and it dawned on me. *Why do I need that from Him?*

Realizing that my thoughts had been foolish, I told the Lord I didn't need to have Him do something to get me to listen. "You know me, Lord, and I will do as you ask. You have already shown me so much." So I asked for nothing.

As I walked around the track, I put out my right arm to show God I knew He is walking with me. I could feel His presence as we made our way around the track three times before I put my arm down.

It was a very intimate time with my Lord, and it would not end there. About two weeks later, I was praising God during our Church Service, and I felt an arm placed directly on my shoulder from the right side of me reaching around and resting on my left shoulder.

Since I was on the end of the pew I looked right and there was no one in the aisle. I looked left and my wife was there, but her arms were beside her. It was my Comforter, my Keeper, my All in All who was there. I lifted my arms in praise to the Lord, and when the song ended and His hand left my shoulder, I went down to my knees and sobbed. I had just felt the touch of God in a way I had never experienced before. I cried as a child who has been lost and then was found and was so joyful that he would do that for me.

For some of you reading this, you may also want something like that to happen to you too. Let me encourage you that when you live a life fully committed to God, you will have experiences that will change your life.

He will teach you and guide you every day of your life. We serve an awesome God, and He desires a personal relationship with us all. We just need to want it more than anything else. Praise God from all blessings flow. Oh how I love You, Lord!

WORDS

You want what you don't have, so you scheme and kill to get it. You are jealous of what others have, but you can't get it, so you fight and wage war to take it away from them. Yet you don't have what you want because you don't ask God for it. And even when you ask, you don't get it because your motives are all wrong—you want only what will give you pleasure (James 4:2-3 NLT).

As I sit writing this chapter, many words have been going through my mind. You see one thing I have learned is words do matter. Words can do powerful things. They can destroy lives or build them back up. They can draw people closer to God or push them farther away. Words matter more than most people think.

The verse above is very much like what the world does to get ahead and often how they go after things. The sad part is that many Christians do the same thing. We ask with the wrong idea of what is best for us. We look for the next great thing that will satisfy our needs. We miss out on much of life, pursuing our own pleasures instead of God's.

I can remember saying such hateful things to someone once that as the words came out, I knew it was wrong and apologized immediately, yet the damage was already done. I had hurt someone's feelings so badly that it would take years to restore that relationship.

On the other hand, it has been my pleasure to see people healed from blindness and deafness, and the lame get up and walk, by one word that was spoken. And the word that is the most powerful word that has ever been is Jesus. In His name we can do all things because He has promised if we are in God's will that it will happen if we would only ask.

The faith I have in God has come because I have stepped out in faith many times and found out that we cannot "out ask" God, nor confine Him to a box that restricts His movements in our lives when He wishes to move.

He is a big God and can do all things. He spoke at the beginning of creation and it was so. In other words God said a word and it was done. God can still do anything with just speaking a word.

In the verse above, James mentions the most common problem with prayer is not asking or asking for the wrong things or for the wrong reasons. So the question is when talking to God, are you asking Him to satisfy your desires? Are you just looking for a yes from God or are you pursuing His ideas for your life?

When we come to the Father asking for His help, He is like an earthly father who just wants what's best for his son or daughter. He would give anything for them, but he also knows giving them everything they ask for will not be good for them, so he gives what they need to flourish and grow up to be the person he envisions them to be.

And yet our heavenly Father does even more since before we were even born, Christ died for us so that we might live and have a life worth living. God is the One who created all we see and all we touch and all we smell. He is the One who made us, knows everything about us, and even knows our hearts. There is nothing hidden from Him.

As we go to the Father to ask for anything, we must go

before Him with a mindset that we will accept His perfect will for our lives and live that life as His life not ours. When we do that, He opens doors to the impossible, He shows up in ways we could have never imagined, and the peace of God, which goes beyond all understanding, is with us always, even to the ends of the earth.

May we always ask with a pure heart and with a mindset that we can do all things through Him who strengthens us. And may we ask for anything in His name and He will do it because we have come to God with His intentions and will in our mind before we even get there.

Words do matter!

FORGIVENESS

One of the most important aspects of knowing God is forgiveness. Many have questioned why. It is the one thing that we need from God in order to have a relationship restored with Him after Adam sinned.

God is a righteous God and He does not sin. When man sinned, it separated us from the righteous God who created us. That separation meant death to us.

Through the years after Adam and Eve sinned, man had to sacrifice animals for the atonement of sin in their lives. These animals were the best ones that people had, as an example of the One who would come eventually to take on that sin and pay the cost of it, which is death.

For the Christian, animal sacrifices stopped with the death and resurrection of Christ. God's Word says without the shedding of blood there is no forgiveness of sin, for this is His plan since life is in the blood and the blood covers a multitude of sins. John wrote in John 1:29,

The next day John saw Jesus coming toward him and said, "Look, the Lamb of God, who takes away the sin of the world!"

This tells us that the sacrifice of Jesus on the cross was what we needed to have a relationship with God. That sacrifice was once and for all time. Acts 10:43 says:

All the prophets testify about him that everyone who believes in him receives forgiveness of sins through his name.

After Christ's death and resurrection, John wrote the following passage:

Only through Jesus Christ can one be saved for He said, "I Am the Way the Truth and the Life and no man comes to the Father (God) except through Me (John 14:6).

Now for us that are living today, Matthew 6:14-15 says:

For if you forgive other people when they sin against you, your heavenly Father will also forgive you. But if you do not forgive others their sins, your Father will not forgive your sins.

This passage speaks of how we are to live. We as followers of Christ are to forgive as the Father forgives. Think about that. We were not in a good place with God when He chose to forgive us. Yet He sent Jesus to do just that.

So what is our response to Jesus' sacrifice for us? Is it to forgive those who have hurt us? Are we to truly love our enemies? The answer is yes we are, and it can be very tough to do and love them as if nothing happened.

God not only forgives but He forgets. He separates our sin from us as far as the east is from the west. In other words when He forgives, it is forever. We are to do this also and if we don't, His Word says there will be consequences for us.

On April 22, 2014 I experienced the forgiveness of God. It was Easter Sunday and it was in the morning service at my church. When the offering was taken, I remembered I had left our checkbook at home and had nothing to give.

Knowing the importance of that day and significance of it, I was moved to tears. I told God I was so sorry for not having an offering to give Him that morning, and in that moment something wonderful happened.

God said, "I forgive you, John." Then as God watched me still agonize over the forgetfulness, He again spoke to me and encouraged me. God said, "You are feeding and caring for those I love this afternoon—this pleases Me."

He reminded me of what was going to take place in the afternoon at church. Every year we open the church up to feed and fellowship with those who have no place to go during the holidays of Thanksgiving, Christmas, and Easter. My mom used to be in charge for many years and now I have been given that ministry.

God had looked at my remorse about not having an offering and not only did He forgive me but also gave me my joy back by showing me what was to come that day and how I would be able to serve Him.

It was not about making up for my sin but about forgiving me and showing me that He still loved me, He still had a plan for me. Restoring my relationship back with Him allowed me to again be available to His leading.

I am so thankful that God loves us. He loves you! He loves you! Yes, He loves you! And with that love came through forgiveness on the cross, through His Son Jesus.

THE JEWISH BIKER

This title sounds funny to you I'm sure, but as you will see from the story, it is correctly titled. It was a day that would cause me to reexamine my own values and worth and learn not to think too highly of myself in the process.

I got off work on a nice sunny day about 6:30, and there was a slight breeze coming from the west. The thought of jumping on my motorcycle was tugging on me, so I set off to drive around a little while to relieve some stress from a long day's work.

I was driving along when I felt God tell me to head out of town to the west. I turned around and followed His instructions. As I got a few miles out, I asked God how much farther, and He said, "Keep going." It was kind of exciting to be on such an adventure, and onward I went.

After going over the last hill five miles out of town, I saw a man on a bicycle. What a sight to see! He was a long bearded fellow who looked pretty old, and as I turned my bike around, I could see he was struggling to get up the hill.

I felt God telling me to give the man a ride to town, but I only had my motorcycle so I went back to town, got my son's truck, and headed back out to give him a ride to town. As I approached him, he was now pushing his bike and looked worn out. I stopped and asked if he needed help. We could see a huge storm brewing behind us, heading our way so he said, "Yes indeed" and we loaded his bike and belongings into the pickup and headed to town.

As we drove he said he was sixty something and that he was biking from Deadwood, South Dakota, to Minneapolis, which is over 600 miles. That drive is for the young and not a man who is out of shape and never attempted to bike like this before. He had just jumped on his bike and went for it, not knowing the winds and weather South Dakota is famous for.

He was extremely grateful and in our conversation mentioned he was a new believer in Christ and a Messianic Jew. It had been three years since he became a follower, and he said he was still learning who God is. I told him we will never stop learning about God while we are still on this earth.

When we got to town, we headed off to the free camping site the town had set up. It had showers, bathrooms, cooking grills, and soft grass on which to set up tents. I helped him get unpacked and set up before the storm, told him where my grocery store was, and asked him to stop by in the morning. He said he would and I took off for home.

After dinner I noticed a huge storm outside and didn't think much about it when I headed off to my devotions. It had been a good day and I got to help someone in need. As I began to read, I felt a sickening sensation in my stomach, and God criticized my decision of setting up his tent and leaving him there.

Sure I had helped the man, but what my heavenly Father wanted was for me to take the new believer into my home for the night, to get him out of the storm.

Whoa, I had missed the boat on that one. I had thought I had done so well in my eyes that day and found out later I was dead wrong. Jesus said to do unto others as you would have done unto you, and I sure would have wanted out of that storm. The storm was now over and it was late, so I prayed for him and for the next morning when I would see him again.

The next day I got to work early in case he would want to start out early. As I did my morning Bible time, my prayers were that I would see him again. He did come down to the store for some breakfast and supplies. As we talked, I apologized to him. He told me he was scared during the storm and wished he had made different plans to travel, but insisted on pressing on.

I gave him his supplies, something else to help him on his journey, and a card with my phone number and address in case he needed someone to come and help him. As he departed, we hugged and he set off on his trip with a big smile and waving as he headed out.

That day I learned to lean on Jesus but also to listen to God's directions better and not to think too highly of myself. Pride instead of humility will cause us to stumble and be ineffective for Him. He wanted to take the man out of the storm, and I just moved him to a different location, where he still was out in the storm. I had patted myself on the back and said, "good job." The lesson for me was to not feel too highly about myself and serve others as if I were serving the Lord.

MONEY FOR GAS

One year I was driving home from Nebraska when I got to a gas station on the interstate near Vivian, South Dakota. It was a long day and I was ready to get home. I had my new relationship with God back then and seemed to be always trying to hear His voice. On that particular day I heard Him tell me to do something that would impact me for some time to come.

After I filled the car up with gas and paid for it, a man in his 70s or more asked to talk to me. He said his RV had broken down and the mechanic fixed it, but now he had no money for gas to get back to Rapid City, South Dakota. God prodded me to help him, so I reached in my wallet and gave him everything I had left. That included the money I was going to buy a soda with.

I gave up on the idea of having a drink and gave the money to the man and his wife, but the interesting part of this story was not my act of kindness. It was the fact that another man came up and asked me what I had just done, with a look of condemnation for it.

I told him I gave him money for gas, at which point the man asked if I thought he was taking advantage of me or if I thought it was really going to be used for gas. Puzzled I asked if the man whom I gave the money to had actually gotten his RV fixed there and he said yes he did. The man had already checked the RV place after being asked for gas money from him also. So I asked why he thought he was taking advantage of me. He really didn't have a good answer but just felt he was ripping me off.

I told him I felt God telling me to help the man and I did. If he ripped me off, there will be a day we will all stand before our Maker and have to make an account of our lives. I told him if he did rip me off, a review of his life would point that out and that God would deal with him as he felt necessary. I said my job was to reach out to the lost, hurting, and people in need and help them the best way I can.

I felt compelled to ask the man if he had given any money to the poor man but didn't ask. I just said to him if he too were asked for money and didn't give anything to this needy man that someday he too would be judged for not helping him.

The man walked away upset with my lack of caring if the story of the man with the RV were true or not. I turned and got in my vehicle and was content with just doing what I felt was right.

Since that day I continue to look for opportunities to serve others and not judge the need for what I think it is but from the perspective God wants to show His love. If I can help show that love, I will do the best I can to bless them in their time of need, so that they can get a small glimpse of God in that unselfish act of giving, loving, caring, and serving others.

"Then the King will say to those on his right, 'Come, you who are blessed by my Father; take your inheritance, the kingdom prepared for you since the creation of the world. For I was hungry and you gave me something to eat, I was thirsty and you gave me something to drink, I was a stranger and you invited me in, I needed clothes and you

clothed me, I was sick and you looked after me, I was in prison and you came to visit me.'

"Then the righteous will answer him, 'Lord, when did we see you hungry and feed you, or thirsty and give you something to drink? When did we see you a stranger and invite you in, or needing clothes and clothe you? When did we see you sick or in prison and go to visit you?'

"The King will reply, 'Truly I tell you, whatever you did for one of the least of these brothers and sisters of mine, you did for me'" (Matthew 25:34-40).

TWO OF MY SONS

My sons are now all followers of Jesus, but at one time two of them had no interest in God whatsoever. This is the remarkable story of how God changed their lives, and both came to accept Jesus as Lord of their lives on the same day.

As Christians we all want our family to come to the place where they too are followers of God. I have wanted that for my children since the day they were born and even before that.

Several years ago I set out to help my sons come to know God. The older children knew God, but my youngest two boys were not interested in Him, so I set out to change them. I picked out some scripture to pour over with them and with the help of my wife, I called them to the dining room to do the devotion together.

Within a few minutes I could see that they weren't listening to anything being said, and my heart was torn apart. As tears began to fall, I asked them to look me in the eyes and made the statement: "Jacob and Joshua, I would be willing right now to go outside and be shot dead if you would come to know the Lord like I know Him."

I paused and Jacob said, "Are you done yet, Dad? Can we go now?" I told them they could and they left the room. My wife and I began to cry when this all took place. At the time I did not know God was watching this all play out.

Within hours God told me I was going to give Jacob my new Jeep. It was very nice and it was red. I had saved up to get it and when God said that I was going to give it up to Jacob, I said: "I am not going to give that selfish kid anything." God said: "You will when I call for it." I said: "Okay, I will when you want it, Lord."

Months and months passed and one day my youngest would be freed from evil and give Jesus his life, and with all his excitement he wanted to tell his brother Jacob what had happened that day. We waited for Jacob to come home from school with my wife and a friend named Albert.

After school Jacob came home and went straight downstairs to set up a new TV he bought and play a game on his PlayStation. He didn't know we destroyed several of the games he liked and that I got some money for him to cover the price of those games.

I asked him to come back upstairs to hear Josh's testimony. At that point Jacob saw some games were gone and was very upset. He listened to almost nothing that was said and what Josh told his brother with excitement was met with a look of "I don't care."

When Josh finished speaking, I tried to reason with Jacob to no avail. At that point Albert said: "John, he is not listening right now; let's just close this time out in prayer." I said okay and we began to pray.

As Albert prayed he said to Jacob: "I know what you want. God just told me." Albert stopped and looked Jacob right in the eye and said, "I don't know if you can have it because it is not mine to give, but I know what it is you want. It is red and it has wheels."

Jacob said later that in his mind he thought that Albert was going to say something like if we give him the money for the stuff it will be okay or something along those lines, but

Jacob said he thought: *The only thing that would make me believe that there really is a God would be if my dad gave me his Jeep.*

As soon as Albert said red with wheels, I tossed Jacob my keys to the Jeep. I told him that God told me months ago that I would need to give him my Jeep. "It is all yours, Jacob, just as God said for me to do."

With that Jacob said to Albert: "How did you read my mind?" Albert said that God told him so that he could know God like the rest of us do—as our Lord and Savior Jesus Christ, the Lord of our lives.

That day God brought both of my sons to Himself and changed their lives forever. One was given freedom and the other knowledge that God knows all things. Both boys had unique experiences that helped them know God the way that would bring them to Him and set them both on a course to serve the One who saved them—a day I will never forget.

GOD SPEAKS

After the day I gave my Jeep to my son, my immediate need was for something to drive. My wife used our van and I was left with my old car and a delivery truck. Both have some problems but are drivable. For the next two years I drove those vehicles because they were paid for, and we didn't have the money to buy another vehicle with the two older kids in college.

During the summer I drove the car and in the winter the truck. During the fall, while I was still driving the car, the driver side door began to not open. I tried to get the door fixed by taking it to a mechanic, and when that didn't work, I even tried taking off the door and working on it to no avail. I wasn't able to get it fixed, so I just continued to drive it that way.

One day I was heading off to work and went to get in and forgot the door didn't work so I crawled in the passenger side and made my way to the driver side. I was upset, wondering about how long I had to go without a decent vehicle to drive. The vehicle was a stick shift to make it even worse.

Under my breath I said, "Stupid car! I can't stand it anymore. Why do I have to drive this thing?" I was getting mad and out of nowhere God spoke to me. It was the clearest God had ever spoken to me and without a doubt in my mind it was Him.

God said, "John. you said you were willing to be shot dead if your sons came to know My Son! All it cost you was your Jeep; now quit whining and go to work."

Wow, what an incredible moment for me! You see at the time that I was pleading with my sons to know Jesus, God was watching and He responded by drawing my sons to His Son. I was not praying to God that day I did devotions with my sons. I was just trying to teach them about Him so that they would want Him. God clearly showed me that He honored my sincere plea for my sons, by having both come to know Him on the same day.

As I drove on to work that day, it deeply humbled me and my attitude changed immediately. Never did I complain about the car again. In fact the message God gave me was passed on to many others as an encouragement to them that God is watching as we serve Him throughout our lives.

A good friend came to me a short time later and asked what good did it do me to give up my Jeep to my son. What did I get out of it? "Your son got the Jeep, but you got nothing," he said.

I replied, "My son came to know the Lord because of that event, but even if you take that away. I have learned a lot from not having that Jeep."

He said, "How so?"

"Well, it has been two years now, and the car and truck have no air conditioning, the music doesn't work well, and they are not in very good shape to drive far, but you are missing something."

He said, "What am I missing?"

I said, "How much do you think I will appreciate a new car when I get one?"

He said, "I bet you will appreciate it more than almost any other one you ever owned."

"That's right. I will and if I would have just gone out and

got another one at the time, I wouldn't have appreciated it like I will now. So God is teaching me to be thankful for what I have, and any needs He will take care of."

That special day gave me a moment that will continue to remind me to be thankful all the days of my life. That day helped me see how God provides for me every day. Sometimes He provides us with the answer to our needs even if we haven't ask Him directly about them.

One of those ways was to save my sons by knowing His Son. Thank You, Father, for Jesus and thank You for saving my sons through Your Son.

THE BREAKFAST

As I awoke I was very excited about what was to come. It was February 3, 2012 and I was thinking about my upcoming trip to Africa and what God was going to do there. I was also thinking about taking my friend to Aberdeen to the airport to send him home to Texas. It was 2:50 am.

We left at 3:30 to get to the airport, which is 100 miles from my home. The other thing that made it a special day was that it was the day I would be able to eat again after a fast of seven days. It had been a hard fast and the last day is always the hardest for me. I was anticipating eating and also wondering if my closeness to God would change when my regular schedule resumed.

After getting to the airport, checking him in, and waiting for the flight, it drew close to 6:00 am. After he was on the plane, I headed to breakfast. The restaurant would be open then and probably not busy yet. My stomach began to turn and I could almost smell it.

I got there and waited 10 minutes to get seated as the waitress was getting things going for the day and there were only two customers seated. But I was patient, since I knew the first bite was coming.

I ordered water, coffee, a spinach veggie plate, and a fruit cup. I have learned not to eat meat or starches coming out of the gate after a long fast. The other fast of 40 days had been just a couple months back.

I began to relax, sipping coffee and reading the paper.

When the food came it smelled wonderful, and as she placed it in front of me a man sat at a table straight to the left of me and God began to speak to me, "Here is someone I want you to love for Me." I looked up and heard the manager say good morning and the man seemed cheery. He said it was a nice day and he waited.

I looked at my food and thought I had better begin to eat and forgot about the request. He got his food and began to eat and then I was reminded of what God had said to me.

I looked over and the man was an older man with Parkinson's disease who looked very lonely. His demeanor began to change and I saw his countenance lower as he ate alone.

I decided to give him the paper I just read and he said, "No thanks." I thought, *Let me buy his meal, Lord,* and began to get out my money when I noticed he had already paid and was leaving. I took my last bite and got up and paid for my meal quickly.

I ran to the parking lot to speak with him and caught up without him seeing me. I said in a very happy voice, "I hope you have a wonderful day and may it go well for you." As he continued walking away with his back turned away, he harshly said, "Yeah," as if to say whatever, mister, my life is miserably lonely.

Then it hit me that I was to be an instrument for God to show this man that God cared and have him sit with me or at least have a conversation with him when he was open to it. I had failed.

In the moment my eye was off God to get the food I had craved, God tested me. I cried bitterly, as I drove away from the parking lot. For the next 24 miles till the next town I wept. God was showing me to be ready at all times with sharing the good news of Jesus Christ.

God showed me the man sitting and wondering if anyone cared. His day started with the anticipation of someone greeting him and making the effort to show him love. No one did, except maybe the manager who poured his first cup of coffee.

That food was delicious, but the job God gave me would have been far greater than food in my stomach at that moment. If I would have taken a moment to speak to him, I am sure I would still have gotten to eat that breakfast. I am also sure the fellowship would have been so very sweet and my reward much greater than what I received.

AFRICA, MARCH 2012

As I write today, I realize God has given me much more to write about from my trip to Africa than any other trip so far. It was a time when God was teaching me that He alone will supply my needs, and so it was in Africa.

Some of the letters, thoughts, dreams, and visions will be written in this book so you can see how our God speaks to us. He does speak to those who are ready to listen, to those who are willing to do as He asks, to those who have confessed and taken care of any sin that you can possible think of, and to those God brings to mind for you to take care of.

As a follower of Jesus Christ and a simple man, who has been chosen to do things most men or women haven't experienced, I am truly blessed. It is hard to follow the path God chooses for me at times, but it is always the best path to take.

I wrote down one of the messages given after getting back from Burkina Faso from a conversation I had with God. It made me think upon things of God and what that means for our lives if we truly give up our lives for Him. Here goes:

We have a Savior worthy of all honor and glory and worthy of all our praise. Jesus overcame death. Do you understand fully what that means? He holds the key to life. He is perfect love, He is truth, and He is blameless.

Do you fit into the world like you are a part of the world or is your life so close to God that you are not a part of this world, but just living in it? There is a difference.

Are you being ridiculed or persecuted for your stand for Jesus Christ? If you are, what do you see? Are the hurting drawn to you? Are you producing fruit? Would you leave everything behind if God asked you to? Has He asked you to give up something and you said no? Why? Are God's plans not better?

These were some of the things I have come to appreciate about God. He will call you out and ask you, "What are you doing for Me?" and it will often times be evident the answer is nothing. When we realize this, we had best get back to Him quickly, so you can be of used by Him and strive to live a life worthy of the Lamb.

The Plan for Africa

On February 9, 2012 something incredible and hard to describe with words happened. It started out as any other day, except for the fact I had been asking God to tell me why I was to go to Africa and especially why go alone.

After my workday I went home and down to my exercise room to get a cardio workout. I put in a DVD of a series called "That the World May Know" by Ray Vander Laan and then climbed up on the elliptical machine for my workout.

On the video it showed the place where it is believed John the Baptist was killed. As I watched, tears began to stream down my face from hearing the story that John would not be rescued and would ultimately die there in that place. I was reminded that God's plans are not like what we would think for ourselves.

With no warning something unusual happened. An eerie black cloud came into my basement and covered the TV screen and ceiling lights with a hazy fog. Staring at it for a moment and then realizing it was not of God, I said out loud, "In Jesus' name, leave!" and in an instant it was gone. Almost immediately after that moment, God said, "I have a plan for you in Africa." Then He told me to claim the land that I walk in Africa for Him.

My initial reaction was, "What does this mean?"

I called a good friend who understands dreams and visions much better than I do to ask for her interpretation of that statement God had spoken to me and she said simply, "Ask God." *Duh*, I thought, *how could I have missed that simple thing?* So I hung up the phone and asked God.

As soon as I asked Him to explain what that means, He said, "Take it back again. It is Mine. Set the captives free."

At that moment God also said to pay attention to the DVD that was still running. I saw the time on the screen was at about seven minutes and then He again said, "Pay attention at 17 minutes," as I recall.

The following was what I heard in the video and it touched me to the deepest part of my soul. It was to me from God. I wrote it out, since I knew God was instructing me to pay attention to it. Here is what it said.

God uses human instruments. God expected an 80 year old man to make at least four climbs up the mountain. When you choose to follow the Lord, expect to give every ounce you got in His service. If you obey Me (God), you will be for Me a kingdom of priests.

Priests: those who put God on display. God not only wants people to bring His message, but who will be His message.

And so it is with us. Jesus created a royal priesthood. A people who would be to a broken world the very presence and picture of the God who restores Shalom to His world. Remember how the Lord your God led you all the way in the wilderness . . . to humble and test you . . . to teach you that people do not live by bread alone but on every word that comes from the mouth of the Lord.

Wow! As I stood there I had been attacked by evil and then after it left, God spoke to me. Then I was left with a plan and wrote down what was going through my head immediately afterwards.

This is what I wrote:

As I prepare for the trip, the lines are being drawn. Since I am on the Victor's side, I have no fear. As I look at the world around me, life continues to go on as if nothing will ever change.

You continue to show me change is coming and unless people give up their everything, their lives totally to you, even to the point that every minute is lived for you, they will fail to be who you long for them to be. To die to self. My heart is torn for them.

The task is almost here and I wait upon the Lord for His next move.

From Paris to Ouagadougou

The flight from Minneapolis to Paris was uneventful,

since the seats by me were empty. So I read a lot. The next flight was full and I sat in the very back of the plane next to a woman who said she spoke only French. Figuring I would not have the ability to speak to her, I began to read and then as the flight took off, I noticed her movie screen in front of her was in English, and she couldn't change it to French.

I reached over, tapped on a couple screens, and it switched then to French. She nodded thanks. I nodded back and went back to my reading. For the next 2½ hours we went about our own agenda. A good time later the lady said something to me and it was in English.

The first English words from her mouth were: "I saw you prayed for your food before you ate. What god did you pray to?" I answered: "I am a follower of Jesus Christ. He is God, the Maker of heaven and earth and your Creator."

She said: "Oh, so what are you going to Burkina Faso for?" I took out my Bible and began to show her verses on spiritual warfare and asked her if she believed in evil spirits. She said: "Yes, of course I do."

"Well, I cast them out of people by commanding them to leave in Jesus' name," I told her.

She said, "I would like to see this big thing." She didn't know people could get freedom from evil spirits.

Then I showed her who Jesus is and the plan of salvation. When we got to Romans 10:9 she had me pause a moment after I read it. The verse was,

> *If you confess with your mouth that Jesus is Lord and believe in your heart that God raised him from the dead, you will be saved.*

She then pondered what was read and said: "Let me see

that." I had it all typed out so I handed the passages to her and she asked me to lead her in prayer to accept Jesus. When we finished she said, "You have just made your first Christian." I smiled knowing she didn't know English well enough to know how to say I led her to the Lord.

She told me about her life in France at that point and said the people she knew in France don't believe in Jesus, but she understands it now. "Jesus is my Lord," she said firmly. What a joy to hear her say those precious words!

"You know what?" I said to her.

"What?" she responded.

"The Lord brought me here to speak to you. He knew you would be sitting here today in this very seat, and I would be available to Him to share the good news, so He placed me in this seat next to you to tell you about Him."

She began to cry tears of joy, knowing God had done this just for her. A believer was born that day. I don't know her name, but God does and it is written in the Book of Life.

When we landed she said, "We will probably never meet again, will we?" My response was: "Of course we will, if not in this life then in the life to come." She smiled the biggest grin and got off the plane. So it was how this trip began to take shape for what was to come.

This was the start of my trip to Africa, which was filled with much more than I could ever write in this book. You will get a glimpse in the following sections on that trip.

For those of you who sit on a bus, or ride a plane or subway, as you go about this life, remember to look at those opportunities to share Jesus. You never know when someone will say yes, and you will be so excited to have been there. I have on many occasions gotten to share Jesus with others who either didn't know Him or needed to be encouraged in their walk with Him.

If you declare with your mouth, "Jesus is Lord," and believe in your heart that God raised him from the dead, you will be saved. For it is with your heart that you believe and are justified, and it is with your mouth that you profess your faith and are saved. As Scripture says, "Anyone who believes in him will never be put to shame." For there is no difference between Jew and Gentile—the same Lord is Lord of all and richly blesses all who call on him, for, "Everyone who calls on the name of the Lord will be saved" (Romans 10:9-13).

The Question

The following was from the journal I wrote while in Africa. I had just started my journey, but already I had seen someone saved, someone request prayer for evil spirits to leave, had seen and felt an evil attack on me, and had just seen three angels I had just asked God for. My request for angels was to help and protect me and those people I was with.

It was a bit overwhelming for me to take, but I was walking so close to God that the following words were how I dealt with the extraordinary things I was experiencing in Burkina Faso. Here are those words written below.

The best times of my life have been when I have stepped out in faith, not knowing or fully knowing what I am to do.

What kind of person would do such a thing? Well

I can tell you! A sold out lover of God, a man after
God's own heart, and a person who knows that God
can do all things, for I have seen it, as I walk by faith.

It would be better to be in God's presence and die
here in Africa, than to be at a place where I was comfortable, without trouble and not a care in the world.
What a terrible place to live.

Anyone can go after that life, but a life that is full,
is a life that is filled completely with the pursuit of
God's plan for one's life.

Since knowing His thoughts are not mine, I must
listen for His and follow through with His plans to
the very end.

No, this is not a safe place! No, this is not a comfortable place; and no, I am not complaining. I am in
awe of God for in this place He has freedom to move,
freedom to show His face, to show up and impress
people with His amazing love and power, to show His
amazing grace, the grace that lifts me up from wherever I am.

He sees everything and if we are ready, if we are
wanting Him, and if we are willing to listen, He will
show us who He is.

I AM READY LORD! COME!

*"For I know the plans I have for you," declares the LORD,
"plans to prosper you and not to harm you, plans to give
you hope and a future"* (Jeremiah 29:11).

The Bus

Looking around the bus I was on, I saw a child who was

crying but as he saw me, he stopped crying. I could see in his eyes that this two year old was wondering who this white man was. I see others on this bus, who were also looking back to see who this man was that has boarded their bus.

I wish I had a toy, a treat, something to give the boy, but I have only love to give. When I smile at the people, they smile back, and that is enough to let them know I care, that I wish them well, and that I am happy to be in their presence.

I originally had a small flashlight in my back pack to help at night to watch for snakes when going outside to the bathroom, but I had already given that to the companion sitting next to me. I had mints, but that too was already given away.

Whatever I could find in my backpack to give away, I gave away. I was wishing I had so much more to give. I wanted to bring things, but my friend Phil said it would only give the white man a name that would not be productive. I understood but just wished I could do more. I wished I could give them the joy God has given me, and it could be theirs. I wished my love to serve others would be passed on to them also and that the God I serve would become the God they serve.

Almost everyone so far I met will talk about the god or gods they serve. Most all serve more than one, and some will include Jesus. He is the extra piece, just to make sure. Not their All in All.

My prayer, Lord, is that You would make them want You. Show them who You are in Your Word, in Your deeds, and in and through those who do know You and are completely consumed by You. Keep me close, that I might do Your will and not sin against Thee.

As I sat on that bus, I was reminded of those whom I love

back home. There were many watching what the Lord was doing in Burkina Faso. Many at home were praying and some want to read what I write in the journal I kept as I went about His business. My prayer was, *Show them your love, Lord, through your amazing generous and compassionate nature. Yours is a perfect love and your love must be shown, for you have said they will know us by our love. There will also need to be fruit here so that they can know we are from You, Father.*

By this everyone will know that you are my disciples, if you love one another (John 13:35).

Likewise, every good tree bears good fruit, but a bad tree bears bad fruit. A good tree cannot bear bad fruit, and a bad tree cannot bear good fruit. Every tree that does not bear good fruit is cut down and thrown into the fire. Thus, by their fruit you will recognize them (Matthew 7:17-20).

Thoughts from Africa

This is hard to explain, but I will try. Two weeks earlier God welled up in me in such a strong way that if there was even a hint of any temptation, even a bad thought, God completely stopped it dead in its tracks. Never has this happened to me. I asked specifically that He protect me with His power for this trip as I prepared, and He did.

One night the Holy Spirit moved in me powerfully and showed me more of His plan there. Wow! Another thing the Holy Spirit did was to move quickly into action at a moment's notice. No preparation needed, God supplied my needs. He quickened my recollection of scripture to the point where I had no fear of a question being asked that He wouldn't give me the answer to. He supplied my needs. I know this to be true.

I also felt an attack one night in my room by false bed bugs biting me. I recognized they weren't real bugs and commanded the attack to cease in Jesus' name. Immediately it stopped. Upon this taking place, I asked for angels to protect me for His purpose so that His plan would move forward. Many would not believe this, but God sent angels to watch over me. I slept in perfect peace with only six hours of rest in a noisy place, where evil is very evident, with culture shock, without sleep to that point for 24 hours. Yet God gave me perfect rest.

His rest is real and so is His love for me, for He shows it to me every step of the way. His love is not anything less than perfect love, unconditional, wonderful, incredible love.

I had wondered why He called me and me alone to come here. Who in their right mind would? No one I know from the west with a view outside of God calling them would wish to come here, but the presence of His Spirit makes it worth life or death itself. He reigns in the hearts of man who long to hear from their God and are not afraid to lay it all down for Him.

I pray if anyone reads this, that they will get one point— give it all up for the King! Then He will give you back more than you could ever imagine, and what He gives will last forever. Give it up! All, every part! Hold nothing back! And if you will do this, you will see God.

But the Advocate, the Holy Spirit, whom the Father will send in my name, will teach you all things and will remind you of everything I have said to you (John 14:26).

It Is Well With My Soul

Unless you have been on a mission trip, you will probably not fully understand this section. When we are serving in a foreign land, there are some things that will draw you to God.

You are in a different culture, with different ways of how things work. You have an increased feeling of dependence on God's leading, and you should want to strive to remain pure, righteous, and holy, so He can use you. You lean on God harder than in your everyday life. I have found the two closest times I have been with God have been going to Nepal and Burkina Faso. The only other times would be during deliverance of people from evil spirits.

God is very evident and His hand in leading is also quite distinctive. I do not take a step without His presence felt. I feel it when I am near evil, and I have been blessed to be accompanied by angels and have thanked God for them. They were necessary for this journey.

I have seen evil flee when they come near to me. No language barrier is present with them. They see all children of God, and when we are pure, righteous, and holy, the demons are fearful.

Praise God for even in the presence of evil we can have great joy. This is hard for me to put into words, but I have no fear, none. I do not have any anxiousness or trepidation, only a heart to do what God is asking of me.

It is almost too easy at times. Just live right before our Maker and His plan is revealed.

Therefore, preparing your minds for action, and being sober-minded, set your hope fully on the grace that will be brought to you at the revelation of Jesus Christ. As obe-

dient children, do not be conformed to the passions of your former ignorance, but as he who called you is holy, you also be holy in all your conduct, since it is written, "You shall be holy, for I am holy (1 Peter 1:13-16).

Sitting with God is the best, the safest, and most exciting place to be. I have had the privilege of being right in the front row, watching Him perform great miracles. It's like going to a circus or cool event and then going home and getting to explain all that you saw.

Yes, people can and do appreciate what you tell them, but it is never the same as experiencing it. People who have gone on a mission for God and have been deeply moved get it. They cry with you and rejoice in what you saw much better than those who have not been on a foreign mission trip.

Lord keep using me. Use me until I have nothing left to give. Move me, for this restores my soul and draws me ever closer to You.

The Vision

Nine months after I got back from Africa, my friend Phil called to tell me that he knew what the vision I shared with him was. He wanted to share it with me when he got back to the United States, so I would have to wait a while longer.

The vision went like this: I saw a long line of Africans lined up side by side. They were tied together in some way by a rope and with tree branches. As I watched they were afraid of the evil before them and had no hope.

After I passed them I headed down a narrow road and one by one as I looked back, they were released from the line and began to go down the same path I was on. That is most of the vision God gave me before I went to Africa.

When Phil came back to the United States, he spoke at my church and told us what the vision meant. He had waited till he could share it with me and the whole congregation. I was crying the whole time Phil spoke because I was finally getting to hear what it all meant, months after I had come home, wondering if I would ever know.

In the old days there were slave traders who would come and capture Africans and take them away to be sold as slaves. They would usually grab a person or two from a village while no one was looking and hurry away, hoping to get away without being caught.

When someone did notice, the village where the person was captured would often get a group to go look for them and if they came upon those who had taken their people, they would make a decision. Sometimes the decision would be to fight, but they could lose more people than were taken if they did that. They could also look at the person and if they were valuable, they could trade someone of less value for them, and lastly they could just walk away from the fight and let them be taken.

Phil said he drew my visions on two sheets, and as he was gazing upon them, Pastor Madou walked in and saw the drawings. He said to Phil that it was a picture of the story of his people. "How did you know our story for that picture?" he asked. Phil said, "John told me." Then the pastor asked, "How did John know it?" Phil said, "You know how" and the pastor said, "It was God who told him, wasn't it?" "Yes it was," Phil said.

Pastor Madou went on to explain that story and as they examined it, they said they would use that story to explain salvation to the local people. They had no way of explaining the cross to the people in that culture that made any sense. They said they could now explain how Jesus wanted to save them, so He took their place on that line and released them from captivity as a substitute for them. They would understand the salvation message when Pastor Madou took the pictures to show the others who have yet to hear of Jesus. They had been struggling for an explanation of Jesus dying on the cross for their sins and hadn't found a good way for them to understand what He did for us.

I was deeply touched and still am for the privilege of bringing God's vision to Phil and then from Phil to Pastor Madou. Today that vision is what is being used to help reach an unreached people group half way around the world from where I live with an understanding of what it meant for them when Jesus died on the cross for us all over two thousand years ago.

Isn't it cool how God would take a grocer from South Dakota, give him a vision for Africa, have him invited to come, and then enable him to share the plan of salvation with them through their rich history so that they could understand the gospel of Jesus Christ. Only God could line up such a thing and only God should get the glory for this thing that He has done.

EVIL

I do not want to devote much time to this subject, but it is real, it is around us, and for some it is controlling their lives. The only reason to take the time to talk about evil is that there is hope in Jesus Christ.

Jesus' name alone will cast out evil, and His precious blood was shed for you and me, so that we might live. It is also by His blood we are cleansed from sin.

This is the message we have heard from him and proclaim to you, that God is light, and in him is no darkness at all. If we say we have fellowship with him while we walk in darkness, we lie and do not practice the truth. But if we walk in the light, as he is in the light, we have fellowship with one another, and the blood of Jesus his Son cleanses us from all sin (1 John 1:5-7).

If you look at the world around us, it is easy to see it is broken, and with every day there seems to be more and more incidents that seem more vile, degrading, and impossible to imagine as actually happening, yet they are.

When Adam and Eve sinned, it was the beginning of the end for us. The relationship with God changed that day for them and us, but God didn't want that relationship to remain broken with us so He sent His Son to save us.

Jesus lived a perfect life and was sinless, yet in the end He was sentenced to die for us. The good news is Jesus didn't stay dead—He rose from the dead. Death was overcome when Jesus came back to life.

I have stood in front of evil and it is not a pretty sight, but when Christ is with you, I can tell you firsthand that there is no fear for perfect love casts out all fear. The enemy knows that God won when Jesus conquered death on the cross.

For God gave us a spirit not of fear but of power and love and self-control (2 Timothy 1:7).

The above verse sums it up very well. If you are struggling with fear, remember that God does not give us that fear. Satan is the one who wants to cause you to have fear and become powerless to live a life of freedom. That verse also says God gives us power—the ability to love and have self-control. When you are controlled by fear, it makes your life difficult to live. It has become clearer each day that the closer to God you are, the more peace you have along with the ability to love unconditionally.

When you end this day, my prayer would be that you would cast all your fears on the Lord and let Him have them. You can be free from the grasp Satan has on your life, no matter how big or small that it is, and you can be set free.

Just ask in Jesus' name for that freedom in Christ and watch what happens. If you just can't get to that place alone, but still want that freedom, then gather some brothers and sisters in Christ together to pray with you.

For where two or three gather in my name, there am I with them (Matthew 18:20).

That verse has been proven true over and over in my life. When I get a friend or two together and pray, it seems like doors just fly open and God begins to do the impossible.

We need one another and we are to help one another, so

please don't wait. Just call a friend now to pray for you and let God show you what He can do in your life today.

There will always be evil in this world until God sends Jesus back to deal with it once and for all. But for now we will have to live in a world that is not ours as a Christ follower. Jesus said He has overcome the world, so we must trust in Him to free us in this life from the evil that comes against us.

I have told you these things, so that in me you may have peace. In this world you will have trouble. But take heart! I have overcome the world (John 16:33).

OBEDIENCE

When reading God's Word, you will notice God has given us instructions on His plan for us. Some are easy to see because the world has heard them already, such as the Ten Commandments. Others are to love the Lord your God and love your neighbor as yourself.

While some speak of how to handle money, other verses speak about running from temptation. If we take God's Word and apply it to our lives, we will live a life radically different than what we would have lived apart from God.

So the question I ask today is, Why would we obey God? It is because it will go well for us because His ways are better than ours. His promises are true and when He says something is better, we can trust it is.

For some people, giving up their heart's desires for obedience to God seems like a fool's choice, but it is not. The wise will choose to follow the instruction of the One who made them.

In God's instructions to us He says we must live as Jesus did. When you read God's Word, you will come to a place where you understand that better. As you strive to live as Christ lived, you will see your life transformed from the old you to the new you.

Obedience is not an option for the Christian living for God; it is a command.

The world and its desires pass away, but whoever does the will of God lives forever (1 John 2:17).

What is God saying here?

Jesus' call to the disciples and to us is to imitate His self-denial to allow God to reign supreme in our lives. We are to have no other gods in our lives, and Luke 9:23 says,

If anyone wishes to become my follower, let him deny himself, take up his cross daily and follow me.

Jesus showed us how He obeyed His Father above anything else that He could have chosen to do. Jesus strived to live the way the Father wanted for Him throughout His entire life and never disobeyed the Father.

Since the day I chose to obey God and give all parts of my life over to Him, nothing has remained the same. My desires are to please Him, and when that change came, I became a man after God's own heart. My desire is to please Him by following the plan He has for me.

I can look back now and say if I wouldn't have followed God's plan for my life, I wouldn't have experienced the same joy, pain, love, suffering, patience, adoration, gladness, peace, or any of the other many emotions we have in this life.

When you look at the list and see pain and suffering, you might want to know why it is there. It is because when God has been with you through all the pains of someone dying or a health setback that seems impossible to overcome, you will feel the presence of God in a way you would probably not have without that suffering.

When I have seen men stop smoking, drinking, or doing drugs apart from God, there is a difference. Those who come to know God and tackle these issues with God by their side have it better. When someone dies that knows the Lord, you see them die in peace.

I have seen people with terminal cancer have joy right up until death and at death's door that joy increased because they knew they were going home. I have seen the opposite when fear overtook someone dying who didn't know God, nor what was going to happen to them when they died.

When you live a life of obedience to God, there is a comfort that comes that makes life worth living. When you follow the plan God has for you, then you see His handiwork and understand His love for you better. When you obey Him, you will often times see later on why He asked you to do the task He gave you to do.

I love looking back and seeing how God brought me through something. The night I gave my life to God was the night when I had been feeling that life wasn't worth living. That night was when I finally hit the lowest point in my life and cried out to Him, He freed me from the chains that bound me and gave me life.

The very next day I obeyed God and rid my home of alcohol and filthy magazines. I got rid of anything that I felt God wanted out of my life. I began to read my Bible every day. I became committed to not only going to church, but to helping others and serving in whatever way God wished of me. In that obedience I began to see God radically transforming me.

If you are a Christian living out a life that is not what God wants for you, then I would urge you to change. I would plead with you that the choice you make to obey or not obey God will have eternal consequences.

It will not be an easy life to obey the One who made you, but it will be the wisest choice you will ever make. This life is fleeting and pass quickly; for some people, today will be their last here on earth. Choose this day whom you will serve. If you say, "I will tomorrow," then you have already chosen. *We know that we have come to know him if we keep his commands. Whoever says, "I know him," but does not do what he commands is a liar, and the truth is not in that person. But if anyone obeys his word, love for God is truly made complete in them. This is how we know we are in him: Whoever claims to live in him must live as Jesus did* (1 John 2:3-6).

RELATIONSHIPS LIKE PAUL'S

When we go through life, we develop relationships with people from a variety of different places, cultures, and beliefs, and it can be life changing. Just think about the place where you live right now and what if you have never been anywhere other than that place.

There are places in this world where people have about a five mile area in which they travel around their entire life. They are born, live life, and die in that five square mile area.

Then there are those who have never left their state, those who have never left their country, and those who have never traveled their continent, and still those who have never traveled the world.

I have traveled around the world and have been to those five mile places. What I have found are people that I have come to love deeply. How can this happen? It is because God had a plan for me to go and bring back the stories of what He is doing in those places, and it has been good.

One thing that has come out of these trips is relationships that have been very precious to me. I pray for them. I call them and speak to them. I Facebook, Skype, and text them because I love them very much.

When they hurt, I hurt. When they laugh, I laugh. Why is this? It is because I have lived life with them where they live and have seen God at work there as we worked together for His kingdom. When you serve alongside someone, you draw closer to them than if you just had dinner together.

As I read scripture that Paul wrote, I see the same thing that has been happening to me. I am in love with these people God has brought me to. Paul couldn't wait to get back to them to see what was happening there and to encourage them to keep on keeping on.

He would write letters to them when he was away and reminded them of what God had taught them when he was with them. He would encourage them to stay strong for Christ or to come back to their first love when they had fallen away. Paul truly cared for them and even at the end of this life requested to see some of them so far away. Paul was a missionary to the world and went through much during that time that was almost beyond what a person would seem to be able to take, yet his memories of those places were good. Why? Because of the people he came in contact with and fell in love with. Those relationships were real and lasted a lifetime. I have had the same thing happen to me.

I wish I was in Nepal, Thailand, Burkina Faso, and Texas every day that I wake up. I miss the people there and pray that God would bless them. I ask God to bring me back and allow me to be a blessing to them in some small way. I see the sacrifice they are making to reach those who don't know Jesus.

I miss them more as time goes by, not less. This is because in those places I have seen God in ways I had never seen Him before, and it changed me forever. God is good all the time and even when the situation seems dire, He is there. In those times or places that seem like death or persecution is so near, God reveals Himself even more. I find in those places a God who can do all things—a God who can move mountains and stop the wind, and a God that is worthy of praise.

In those places my view of God was widened and my prayer became more real. My study of Scripture became daily and what I could understand became clearer.

Even as I write this page I have had to stop three times to cry and think about those I love so dearly. If I never see them again in this life, it will break my heart, yet I know I will see them in eternity, whenever that day comes. Paul had that feeling too, and I am blessed to have known so many here on this earth that few will ever meet.

> *We always thank God for all of you and continually mention you in our prayers. We remember before our God and Father your work produced by faith, your labor prompted by love, and your endurance inspired by hope in our Lord Jesus Christ.*
>
> *For we know, brothers and sisters loved by God, that he has chosen you, because our gospel came to you not simply with words but also with power, with the Holy Spirit and deep conviction. You know how we lived among you for your sake. You became imitators of us and of the Lord, for you welcomed the message in the midst of severe suffering with the joy given by the Holy Spirit. And so you became a model to all the believers in Macedonia and Achaia. The Lord's message rang out from you not only in Macedonia and Achaia—your faith in God has become known everywhere. Therefore we do not need to say anything about it, for they themselves re-port what kind of reception you gave us. They tell how you turned to God from idols to serve the living and true God, and to wait for his Son from heaven, whom he raised from the dead—Jesus, who rescues us from the coming wrath* (1 Thessalonians 1:2-10).

THE PLANE

What started out as any other plane trip changed from an ordinary flight to an emergency landing that gave me a chance to see what few people get to see—the reaction to life possibly ending before your eyes and the eyes of others.

As we left from Denver, to head to Pierre, South Dakota, we fastened our seatbelts and took off with no idea of what lie ahead. I settled back listening to those around me talk of their recent trips. Some trips were to loved ones, others were to conferences, while others went on trips just to get away and relax. As we headed to our destination, our plane began to shake violently and lean to the left in what felt like a hard position for our pilots to maintain. It didn't take long before we knew something was going to have to happen quickly to fix this situation.

After a few minutes of waiting for a response from our pilot, we heard from him that we were going to have an emergency landing in ten minutes or less and that we were trying for Cheyenne, Wyoming. We began our preparation time, as each of us thought about what was about to happen.

I was sitting in an exit row and looked over to the door to see what I was to do in an emergency landing—push the seat forward, pull the lever, and push the door out. After reading this I began my conversation with the Lord. I remember saying that I'll see you in a couple minutes, Lord, or I will still be here on earth. I didn't know which one it would be, but I knew I was ready regardless of the outcome.

As we approached the runway, a lady behind me asked, "Are those firemen and the ambulance there for us that we saw on the end of the runway?" I remember telling her yes, that since we were having an unexpected landing they were there for us as a precaution. We held on and braced for the landing that was to come.

The landing was remarkably smooth, in light of all the swaying we were experiencing. Upon landing the reactions became clear as to what each person thought of this flight. One said, "I told you we should have stayed in Vegas" as he and his friend made a beeline for the airport bar to have a few. Others hugged each other and cried, while others grabbed their phones and called loved ones to tell them what happened. It was on the same night that the Buffalo, New York crash happened and the news was full of it. As we waited in the airport for what was to happen next, someone said, "Shut that TV off. We don't need to see that right now after what we just experienced."

One thing I noticed was not just that I was looking at those around me, but that others were watching also as this landing took place. One lady came up and thanked me for what I did. I had no idea what she was talking about since I didn't have to open the door, so she told me what touched her. She said she took comfort in the fact that as she watched me, I looked at the door to plane and prepared for my task, but more importantly that I bowed to pray and looked up from prayer and stayed calm through the whole situation. That calmness kept her from going over the top and reacting in a way she said would not have helped the situation. This reminds me that people are watching us and our reaction to life's challenges and how we address them.

As time passed and we got on a plane to travel the rest of the way to Pierre, it gave me time to think. I had just gotten to see what my reaction to death would be like at the end of my life. I was ready! Yes I was ready to go if it were my time with no hesitation, no remorse, just "Whatever you wish, Lord, whatever you wish."

I saw that this world has many who are not ready to leave and are poorly prepared to do so if it is their time. This has given me an increased sense of urgency for the lost that I didn't have before—those lives we come in contact with everyday, who don't know that God loves them, would do anything to have a relationship with them, and has done everything to ensure that through giving us His Son Jesus Christ.

If they could only see how God wants to give them everlasting life, and that no matter what comes their way, He will never forsake them or leave them. If they would only recognize and believe that Jesus took the punishment for their sin when He died on the cross and was later raised on the third day.

Looking back at the plane incident that day, the reason I was able to stay calm in that situation was only because God was with me and His Spirit encouraged me there as the plane landed. If not for God, I too would have been very anxious about was what about to happen that day.

Do not be anxious about anything, but in every situation, by prayer and petition, with thanksgiving, present your requests to God. And the peace of God, which transcends all understanding, will guard your hearts and your minds in Christ Jesus (Philippians 4:6-7).

MY FATHER

October 15, 2012 was another day I will never forget. It was the day my father passed from this earth to eternal life with God in heaven. It was an unexpected event as you will see from the story.

Six days earlier my mom and dad signed the papers to sell their half of the store to my wife and me. We were going to have our son James and his wife Jaymi become partners with us, as Mom and Dad were heading out to enjoy their retirement.

On October 13th my family threw a retirement party for my mom and dad with many people coming to say congratulations to them both. Many pictures were taken, and boy did my dad smile. He was ready to head south for the winter to get away from all the snow that was surely coming.

That was on a Saturday and on Monday he came in to check on things. We had a cooler not working right, so he told me what to do and I attempted to fix it. He came over and step by step led me through the process of changing a defroster.

A customer came up and said to my dad that his son had missed his call in life and that I should have been a pastor. I remember my dad stopped what he was doing and said, "No he didn't miss his call. God is using him right where he is and that is what God wants from John, and I am glad John does what God says."

We headed to the office where dad and I worked at every

day and talked for another hour. He had been having heartburn for a week, and it wasn't letting up and he was wondering how long the medicine would take to kick in.

We talked about other things and he headed home to make a map of their big drive to Texas. After he left I went outside to check on the cooler, and a service man drove up and asked what I was doing. I told him and he said I should clean out the coils also, so I called Dad and he said to go ahead and clean them out.

After getting out a garden hose, I noticed that I would need a spray nozzle, so I walked two blocks to the hardware store. Halfway there I heard God say, "Coming home soon!" I said, "What do you mean, coming home soon?"

Am I going to die? Who is going to write the book you asked me to write? I was stunned as I walked and was waiting for an answer. I grabbed the nozzle and the owner said he would charge it to me. I headed right back to the store.

As I reached the store, James and Jacob were outside frantically looking for me, and said Grandma called and that it was Grandpa. *Go to their house now!* I drove the six or so blocks to their house and arrived before the ambulance.

My mom and I performed CPR on Dad until the medics arrived. Then I continued with one of the EMTs helping. They loaded Dad up with my mom accompanying him and got him to the hospital with the rest of us following behind.

He was pronounced dead a short time later. The autopsy said that CPR wouldn't have worked on him as his heart just gave out. What a shock! Retire and a week later you are gone. That night as I sat outside thinking about the day, I understood God warned me what was going to happen when He said coming home soon. An EMT that was there and a good friend called my cell phone and asked why I seemed okay with all that happened.

She said the shock of it and performing CPR on your dad had to cause you great pain and sorrow. I said to her that God had told me what was going to happen before it did. I just didn't know it was my dad who was going home, so I was okay.

After that conversation God again spoke to me and said, "He is with me now."

I got up and went into Mom and Dad's house and told her what God had just said about Dad. She cried and thanked me for sharing that with her.

Later as time passed I told that to someone in our church and they began to cry. As I listened to their story, I too cried because God had done the same thing for them also with a loved one who passed away. A sister said God told her, "Coming home soon" shortly before their father's passing.

God had given them peace the same way God gave my family and me peace during this difficult time. He can do the same for you.

Peace I leave with you; my peace I give you. I do not give to you as the world gives. Do not let your hearts be troubled and do not be afraid (John 14:27).

ASK

On the March 24, 2014 I hurt my back moving a heavy box. In one moment I went from feeling strong to being totally unable to even walk without excruciating pain.

Over the next week it did not get better. I only have access to a chiropractor on Mondays and Thursdays, and it happened so late on Monday that I knew Thursday would have to do. Well, along came Thursday and I had to leave town with my mother to gather some things from a house my grandmother had so that the house could be sold.

That left the following Monday before I would be able to see the chiropractor. Sleeping was becoming unbearable and my days were long as I struggled through the pain. Monday came and the chiropractor was unable to come because of the snowstorm that we were about to experience.

That day about nine inches of snow fell and it would need to be plowed. The next morning at 4 am I got up, dressed, and headed out the door to plow snow, with my back hurting the whole time.

As I finished up plowing my grocery store parking lot, I headed out to my employees' homes to get them plowed before they tried to head to work. I got three done and something odd began to happen.

I saw several widows attempting to move the heavy snow, so I volunteered to plow their snow on that day. God began using me to help first one and then another and then another on that day.

After another hour of plowing, my back was beginning to really, really hurt, and as I was suffering I cried out to God. "Lord, I am hurting and have been plowing out the driveways and sidewalks of the widows you have shown for me to take care of today." Then I asked Him to help me through this pain in my back. I said "Lord, please take away the pain in my back so I can finish doing what You ask of me today."

In an instant the pain was gone. Totally gone! It had been a week of pain and now I could feel nothing. I praised God and continued on with no pain. When finished I went off to work and worked all day like I hadn't been able to before.

Why had God done this? Why was it so quick that He responded? I began to ponder what had just happened and why the healing took place. God knew I was suffering. He sees everything, and I had shared my pain with Him earlier in my prayer time, so why now?

It was because I asked! I was right before my Creator doing what was before me to do and I simply put in a request and He said, "Okay, John. I will heal you!" It was as simple as that. Why all the questions? Why was I so surprised?

I think it is because sometimes we ask without expecting the miracle that will accompany it. That pain being gone allowed me to continue on that day. And it may surprise you but the next day when I got up to start my day, the pain was back.

I wondered why it was back. Was it lack of faith or was it just God's will? It was in that moment of wondering that God showed me why. It was for that moment for me to finish the task. The pain I had been having was serving another purpose, drawing me to a point I could learn another lesson from God.

The fact the pain came back also showed me that it was truly Him who healed me in that moment. Why else would I have that time without pain when it was so severe both before and after?

And I will do whatever you ask in my name, so that the Father may be glorified in the Son. You may ask me for anything in my name, and I will do it (John 14:13-14).

HOLINESS OF GOD

Thinking about God and His holiness has taken me to places I didn't think I would go. Today was a day where the holiness of God was overwhelming, all-consuming, and has left me speechless.

I have sat here in the quiet of my writing room for over an hour, searching for the perfect answer and have not come up with it. I even sat in silence waiting for God to tell me. This too did not come to pass. So here I am, thinking about how to describe the holiness of God.

In searching for a definition I found things like set apart, pure, sinless, speaks truth always, above all else, uncompromising, steadfast, and good, to name just a few.

In Isaiah 6 and in Revelation 4 the angels declare that God is "holy, holy, holy." This caught my attention for where else do the descriptions of God use that kind of emphasis.

Does scripture say that God is a great, great, great God or that He is patient, patient, patient, or that He is love, love, love? No, the only time in scripture that this is found is in the description of God being holy.

So this holiness has significance both in the description and characteristics of God. We find in Revelation 4 that it says and day and night they never cease to say, "Holy, holy, holy, is the Lord God Almighty, who was and is to come!"

In Isaiah 6:3 it says,

And one called to another and said: "Holy, holy, holy is the Lord of hosts; the whole earth is full of his glory!"

This is another passage clearly emphasizing that God is holy. Wow, this word is said day and night before the Lord, so that in itself means that this word is important and describes God well or it would not be taking place like that in heaven.

If I had to come up with some words that would help us with what describes the holiness of God, then I would use words like divine, hallowed, humble, pure, righteous, faithful, good, spotless, just, faultless, upright, and perfect, to name a few.

Because God is holy, when Adam and Eve sinned, there was a separation of God and man. When Jesus died and rose again, it gave us an opportunity to again enter into a relationship with God if we confess our sins and choose to believe in His son Jesus.

It says in Romans 10:9 if you confess with your mouth that Jesus is Lord and believe in your heart that God raised Him from the dead, you will be saved. When we have done that, then we enter into a relationship with a holy God and all three parts of the godhead are holy. the Father, the Son, and the Holy Spirit.

Jesus is described as holy in Acts 4:30, "Stretch out your hand to heal and perform signs and wonders through the name of your holy servant Jesus."

The Holy Spirit teaches us about the Father and the Son and shows us what true holiness is. First Corinthians 2:10 says these are the things God has revealed to us by His Spirit. The Spirit searches all things, even the deep things of God.

So who is like God? Is there anyone as holy as Him? Well God even asked that question in His word. God says in Isaiah 40:25, "To whom then will you compare me, that I should be like him? says the Holy One."

Samuel answers that question in 1 Samuel 2:2, "There is none holy like the LORD: for there is none besides you; there is no rock like our God."

God's Word says that His is not tempted by evil and He is perfect, without sin and flawless. So now that we have a little understanding of what it means for God to be holy, there is another thing we need to know.

We are also called to be holy. What? We are to be holy? Yes, here is some scripture to back that statement up.

I am the Lord your God; consecrate yourselves and be holy, because I am holy. Do not make yourselves unclean by any creature that moves along the ground. I am the Lord, who brought you up out of Egypt to be your God; therefore be holy, because I am holy (Leviticus 11:44-45).

Be perfect, therefore, as your heavenly Father is perfect (Matthew 5:48).

So as you read this chapter today, I would encourage you to take time to review the life you are living and compare it to the God who is holy. If you are not living a life that is pleasing to God then begin today to do just that.

God has called us to live as Christ lived, to give of ourselves in a way that serves others' interests above ours. We are to be holy. That is something we will not have completed in us until we are home in heaven with the One who is holy, but it is what we strive for and will eventually die for. On that day we will see holiness face to face, because God is holy, holy, holy.

YOU WERE BORN FOR THIS

One September my wife and I attended a wedding that was held out in the countryside in a field on a beautiful day. The couple had a large wooden cross up front behind them, so when the wedding was over, I walked up to gaze at the cross.

As I was walking up to the cross, Dan, a friend and uncle of the bride from Omaha, Nebraska, began to talk with me, and during our conversation, he paused and said, "Please follow me."

A bit bewildered I went with him to his van where he handed me a book called, *You Were Born for This*. He told me God said to bring it with him to South Dakota and someone would say some words to him and when they did, he was to give the book to them. He said in our conversation I said the exact words that God told him would be said, so he handed me the book.

I accepted the book and later at my store, I was looking at it, wondering why God had him give it to me. At that point my good friend Tom walked in my office, greeted me, and took a peek at the book in my hand. He said, "What's this?"

After a moment Tom said, "John, you would never have bought that book. Did you look at the author?" It was Bruce Wilkinson, the man who wrote the book called *The Jabez Prayer*.

Tom was right. People who had read the book told me things that made me very uncomfortable. It was all about how this prayer did this or that for them. They told me how all day long they would pray this prayer and how the prayer did remarkable things for them. I was aghast at the time, and it was because almost every person said it was the prayer that accomplished these miracles. It was not the prayers, but God who can do all things; and I felt God was not getting His due for what He was doing in these people's lives. So I didn't buy anything from that author again.

But God did want me to have *You Were Born for This* so He had someone bring it to me. At the time I needed to read what Bruce wrote in that book. It had a huge impact on my life and I still do today some things that Bruce suggested. He wrote words that matched my life perfectly at the time.

That book spoke to me about having incredible things happening and yet feeling alone like there is no one else who understood what you are going through outside of God. I was feeling all those things he was saying.

Later as I listened to that book on CD, it came to a part that said something like, "Are you lonely; do you feel like no one understands what is happening to you?" My wife was sitting next to me reading a book and heard none of what was being said. I felt incredibly alone at the time with much on my mind. Upon hearing those words I began to softly cry while my wife had no idea as she continued to read her book.

Bruce said to put some money in your wallet for God and when God asks for it, then do with it what He asks. I have done that faithfully since the day I read that book, and God has asked for it several times and every time is special. Then I get more money and place it in my wallet for the next time God wants to use it.

God knew I needed to hear the encouraging words in

that book and to know there are others like me that have this wonderful relationship that many don't have. The gift of knowing God as I do moves me often to tears as I think about what He has done for me. I know I am a sinner saved by grace and deserve none of the good that is happening in my life, yet God chose me and wanted a better life for me than what I could have devised myself.

It's not a comfortable life, not a life filled with stuff, but a better life. He always gives me what I need, not what I want. He will give me the desire of my heart if those desires are matching His for my life.

For those reading this book, I would love for you all to have a relationship with God that He intends for you. You were born for a purpose. You were born because He formed you with a plan for you to follow.

"For I know the plans I have for you," declares the Lord, "plans for welfare and not for evil, to give you a future and a hope. Then you will call upon me and come and pray to me, and I will hear you. You will seek me and find me, when you seek me with all your heart" (Jeremiah 29:11-13).

Ask, and it will be given to you; seek, and you will find; knock, and it will be opened to you. For everyone who asks receives, and the one who seeks finds, and to the one who knocks it will be opened. Or which one of you, if his son asks him for bread, will give him a stone? Or if he asks for a fish, will give him a serpent? If you then, who are evil, know how to give good gifts to your children, how much more will your Father who is in heaven give good things to those who ask him! (Matthew 7:7-11).

These verses you just read give us hope and a future. They encourage us to seek out the One who made us and ask for His help in our lives. He promises to give to those who ask and the door will open if you ask. He loves us and tells us that He gives good things. For you were born for this.

More Than We Could Ever Imagine

On October 6, 2012, I boarded a plane flying from Minneapolis to Houston. I was near the back, and as I sat down on the plane and got ready for takeoff, God spoke to me.

He said to give the money I had put aside for Him to the couple in front of me. I looked forward and saw a couple with three children. I took out a piece of paper and wrote a note saying that God told me to give this to you.

After placing the paper and money in my top shirt pocket, I waited for an opportunity to give it to them. As I sat there I began to wonder, *Why them? What had caused God to want to give it to them?*

After the flight took off, all seemed good and we were relaxing in our chairs anticipating our arrival to our destination.

As I sat reading a book, I heard something and looked up. It was one of the children struggling and having a tough time being on the flight so the mom and dad took turns trying to comfort the child.

After some time passed, the child began to cry again and the look on the mom's face stayed with me for some time. She was struggling now too, as she attempted to help their child calm down while our flight continued.

As I went back to my reading, their little girl must have headed off to the bathroom and that is when things got much worse. All of a sudden a stewardess went back to the bathroom to see why the person was in there so long.

The stewardess started banging on the door and yelling, "Get out of there. Come out right now. You better not be smoking in there. Open this door right now." She was so loud and angry that most of us in the back were looking at what she was doing. She was both kicking and pounding on the door as she yelled.

At that point the father came running back because he knew his little girl was in there. When the little girl finally figured out how to unlatch the door and open it, the stewardess pushed it open. The terrified little girl saw her dad and latched onto him, crying fiercely.

After the dad got back to his seat, another child began to cry and before everything calmed down, it looked like the whole family was overwhelmed with everything that had been happening.

I saw the mom begin to cry from all that had just transpired, and at that point God showed me quite clearly that He knew this was going to happen and wanted to give them something to show He loved them.

For the first time in my life, God had shown me how He knows our future, for He had me get the money and note ready before the problem ever arose. At that point I asked if I could add some of my money with His and place it with the note. I wanted to be a part of the plan to encourage this precious family. And God agreed.

So placing some more money with the note was my next step and then after that I waited for an opportunity to present it to them.

When we landed and everyone began deboarding the

plane, I heard the mom say, "Let everyone get off that is be-hind us, and we will gather our stuff and get off last." At that point I realized the note could be passed more easily as I went by them.

When it was my turn to head out of my seat and down the aisle, I got up and as I went by them, I reached out my hand and placed the note and money in the father's hand. He looked up at me and asked what it was for.

I said that God told me to give it to him and quickly left the plane. My gate for the next flight was quite far from where we landed and there was not much time between flights, so off I went, never to see them again.

I don't know what their reaction was upon reading the note. I don't know if they thought I was crazy saying God told me to do that or not, but what I do know is God knows what is going to happen before it happens and that is a com-fort to me.

That gesture showed me how much God cares for us. The fact that He would prod one person to help another was in-credible to me because He already knew they would need that encouragement well before the trouble came.

The following verse shows us that God does know us and also our needs. He has a plan for us and will carry them out, as He wishes.

Before I formed you in the womb I knew you, before you were born I set you apart; I appointed you as a prophet to the nations (Jeremiah 1:5).

That experience is one of those lessons that teach us how God is truly in control of all things. I have thought of them often wondering how they are doing. Even if I never get to meet those God shared His love with that day, I know God knows all things and cares for us in ways we could never imagine.

THE SUNGLASSES

On February 11, 2013 I set out to plow snow. It was 5 a.m. and knowing that in a couple hours or so the sun would be shining, I hung my prescription sunglasses over the sweater I was wearing under my winter coat. I got in my pickup and drove up to the shop to get the tractor to begin plowing snow.

In the alley behind my shop I got stuck in a foot of snow. I got out of the truck and walked up to the shop, got the tractor, came back, and dug the truck out. After getting it freed, I drove the truck to the shop, went back to the tractor and began to plow snow.

I plowed the alley and the parking lot behind the shop to open up the way to drive in and out more easily later on, then I went about my day of plowing.

About 9 a.m. the sun came out, so I reached for my sunglasses. They were gone and I needed them badly. My eyes are very sensitive to sunlight and I began to panic. I pleaded with God to help me find them. Where could they have fallen out, or did I leave them at the store where I was just at.

At that point I was really wondering where to look when God said: "You will have your glasses back." I thought wow and went up to the shop to take a look. After looking all over no glasses were found, and for the next few days I would continue to look.

Had I not heard right what He said? I knew it was God's voice. Maybe I missed something. Why no glasses? He said I would have them back.

By Friday I had given up finding them and set up an eye appointment for the next Friday because the eye doctor would not give me new ones without an eye exam.

On Sunday I headed off to church and had a God-filled morning and left feeling God was with me in a mighty way. It was a service filled with praise to the God I love so dearly, and it was a very good day.

I hopped in my pickup and started backing up to head home when I heard God say: "Go get your glasses."

Immediately I headed off to the alley where I thought they might be. Driving halfway up the alley I stopped. Looking out the window all I could see were ten foot piles of snow and a hopeless situation. I had no idea where to look, so I asked God where to look.

I remember saying out loud: "Where are they?" At that point I was sitting inside my truck when my eyes focused on the snow pile outside my driver's side window and saw something.

Could it be? Could this be my glasses? I thought as I opened the door.

Without even having to step completely out of the truck, I reached out into the snow pile and picked them up. One of my feet was still in the truck.

"Whoa" was my exact word. God's words were true and even made it easy to find my glasses that day. God had given them back to me.

Almost immediately I remembered my optometrist appointment. *Oh John of little faith. Why did you get in such a hurry when God told you that you that you would have them back only a few days earlier?* I can see I have a long way to go with my faith.

God had made a promise to me and when a little time passed, I bailed on Him and went about my own plan to get new glasses. His promise never changed, but my lack of patience was never going to allow time to pass first.

As I get older I see how God's timing is better than mine and we can become impatient with Him. Over and over He has shown me that He is faithful. He is always there for me and never fails me, yet if I do not see movement at times, I make a way to get things done myself.

In those times it seldom goes well and the success rate is very limited. That day when I got my glasses back there could have been an, "I told you so" from God, but all I heard was "Go get your glasses!"

God is not man, that he should lie, or a son of man, that he should change his mind. Has he said, and will he not do it? Or has he spoken, and will he not fulfill it? (Numbers 23:19).

Sanctify them in the truth; your word is truth (John 17:17).

Teach me your way, O Lord, that I may walk in your truth; unite my heart to fear your name (Psalm 86:11).

One lesson I learned was that His word is true. He does not lie and even when we see the things through our skewed eyes it does not change the truth of His word. He cannot lie and does not lie.

When He speaks to us you can know that what He says will happen. When God said Jesus will come back, then Jesus WILL come back. Not may or could come back, but WILL. The promise is true, so as we look for His return, which will happen, we continue to go about His business, anticipating and looking toward to the day we are home with Him forever.

Hold onto God, who is truth. He understands you and when you read or hear His words, remember you can count on them as fact—not a possibility, but something that will be forever true, even if it is simple as you will have your glasses back!

Walking with God

After God gave the sunglasses back to me, I went home to think about it some more. I had recognized my shortfall and wandered why I had failed to wait for Him to come through for me.

That evening I stepped out of my house to go for a walk and experienced something new to me. As I headed down the street the ten or so blocks to the track, where I love to both walk and talk with God, something happened.

About half way to the track, with no light from the moon and with a very dim streetlight, I walked right into a huge pool of water on the corner near my church. The water quickly filled my shoes and went up past my ankles.

The temperature outside was probably in the 30s and the water was icy cold with ice actually floating on it, which made it was even colder.

Upon the initial shock of the water, I realized my time with God would have to be cut short because of my wet feet and the cold temperatures. I was also walking in some snow, and the track would be covered with snow for sure, which meant my feet would be even colder then.

At that point I asked God for the impossible. I asked

God to dry my feet in Jesus' name, and it happened in an instant. I had paused on the other side of the waterhole and asked God and He said yes.

My feet were completely dry and the warmth that came instantly to my feet was a testament to the power of Jesus name and the love of the Father.

As I continued on, God taught me another lesson. When I reached the track, I was given instructions. At the beginning of the track, I saw much snow and very little light to see where to walk.

I stood there and thought about just hanging out there at that spot, when God said, "Walk!" So I started toward the dimly lit part of the track and then God said to go the other way. So I went in the other direction, which was almost completely dark. About one quarter of the way around the track, I asked God how far was I to go and He said, "Walk until you sink in."

About halfway around, I sank deep into the snow that I couldn't see coming, which was up past my knees. At that moment God said for me to remove my head coverings. I had on a snow hat and hoodie, both of which I pulled off the back of my head. Then I took off my headphones at which point my head was bare.

Standing there silent and wondering what was going to happen, I saw and heard a rushing wind come by me and through me, and I felt God's presence.

Then I heard His voice again. He said, "Walk," and I started to walk, but almost immediately He said to turn around and go the other way. I turned around and started back. After about twenty steps I noticed the light was showing the indentations my feet had made earlier.

I started stepping in those holes my feet had made earlier, since the snow was hard to walk on. Then once again God showed me something. (If you have never walked in snow, here is a lesson for you.) Our feet point outward slightly for most people as we walk. As I walked the opposite direction the toes are turned around, so your toes now point inward, so with each step I had to be purposeful in stepping into the hole my feet once were in.

After several steps, God said: "John, you can see it is possible to walk in those steps. It is like that following Me and My plan for your life. When you walk as Christ walked, you can see it is not impossible, but it is very hard."

The lesson for that day was to walk as Jesus walked, knowing it will be difficult but not impossible. We will sin and get off course, but when we are right with God, we can walk as Jesus walked. Thank You, Jesus, for giving us the example on how to live.

Those who say they live in God should live their lives as Jesus did (1 John 2:6).

GOD'S STORE

In 1988 when we bought the grocery store in Gettysburg, we made some immediate changes. We took out all the alcoholic beverages and adult magazines. Where I worked previously I saw the youth stealing the beer and wanted to protect them from that at my store and also from the magazines that were filth.

In 1991 I rededicated my life to Christ and again God moved me toward more changes for both me and for my store. I took out all lottery tickets and began to take out magazines that we felt were not good to have available to our customers—another step of changing to what we felt God would want from us.

But in 2011 God began to open my eyes to greater things, and I could see other problems in the way I ran the grocery store that I called God's store. My family and I would tell people that we felt God had entrusted the store to us to run, and at that time God began to move me to run it as if it were truly His.

So I asked God what I should do differently and to open my eyes to His plan. That prayer came with an immediate response and from that day on there have been some dramatic changes to our grocery. To start with, we removed all cigarettes, cigars, and similar products.

We then began to be closed on Sundays. I took out all secular books and have only Christian books for sale. I took out all secular movies rentals and put in only Christian

DVDs. I have a Christian section of items for sale. I give out gift bags of Christian items on Christmas and Easter to all the children I come in contact with at the store.

We have a display of Christian tracts free to anyone who wants one. I always have a Bible to be given away that will help someone who needs it.

The music has been changed to Christian music, and our offices are filled with things of God. I keep books in my office to give away to the person whom God shows me needs it. I have money in my wallet available for God to give, and the food at the store is always available to be given away.

We pray over the store that God would bless it. I wear a cross that is visible every day. The ballcaps that I wear at work all have Christian sayings. We look for ways in the community to help the down and out. We give, expecting nothing in return. We serve meals for those with nowhere to go on Thanksgiving, Christmas, and Easter.

I am not saying these things because I think I am something special or have it all figured out. I certainly don't think this way and will not have it all right until I am home with the One who made me, but I can change. I can be more like Christ. And that is what I strive to do.

If you look at these choices from the world's view, it is strange. When you take out products your customers want then they usually go elsewhere to get it. The thing about taking a stand for Christ is that it always has a cost.

People say to me, "Well, the Christians will support you." In reality most watch their money and shop where they can get the best deal, so many of them purchase only the specials and shop at many different stores.

I remember on a trip to Promise Keepers on a bus to

Denver, the driver decided it was time to stop so he picked a convenience store and pulled over by it. I went across the street to a different store. When I got back on the bus, I had a friend say to me that it was smart of me to go to the other store because the lines were full at the one the bus stopped at.

I said I went there because that store didn't sell dirty magazines or beer. He said it would have never entered his mind to do that. He just stops wherever. I often see that many Christians don't seek to support those who are trying to live a life pleasing to the Lord. We are not looking to encourage each other by supporting those businesses.

Yet we are still in business. I have had many people come to me over the years because they said I do what I say and am honest in my dealings. My help enjoys working for us, and we have very little turnover outside of retirement. We are blessed to have our employees and the customers we serve.

Yes, we do struggle to make it in this business, but we always strive to live for Christ. When given the chance, we bless those who need it at the time they need it most because that is what we have been called to do.

Finally, brothers and sisters, whatever is true, whatever is noble, whatever is right, whatever is pure, whatever is lovely, whatever is admirable—if anything is excellent or praiseworthy—think about such things. Whatever you have learned or received or heard from me, or seen in me—put it into practice. And the God of peace will be with you (Philippians 4:8-9).

GUN TO MY HEAD

A few years ago on a Sunday night on what seemed like the perfect end to an ordinary day at our house, the phone rang. That call has helped me to have an ever increasing confidence in God.

When I picked up the phone, I heard the words of a distraught parent who had just received a call from her son. He said that he was going to kill himself and that he was sorry. She said, "I don't know why I called you but I did." She asked if I could go over to his house and check up on him before it might be too late. I said yes and asked where he lived. She told me the address and off I went.

I got in my truck and the radio was on. As I listened during the few short blocks to his house, there was a message that hit me like a ton of bricks. It was something like, "Are you ready to go to Jesus if your life ended today?"

I remember thinking that was a strange thing to hear as I was going to help this man. As I got closer I began to ponder the question: What was I going to encounter when I get there?

Upon arrival I went up to the door and began to bang on it and let the man know I was there to help him. I could hear awful music blaring from inside so that he probably couldn't hear me.

At that point a policeman drove up. He got out and put his spotlight on me and saw who I was. He then said: "Go in and get him out." I said okay and went inside. I told him who

I was and again said I was there to help. He heard me and yelled for me to get out of his house. As I went around the corner to enter the room with the loud music where the man was, I wondered what I was going to encounter along the way. I remember looking out the window toward the policeman and seeing him standing outside the house.

As I entered the next room, there he was and I was greeted with a gun aimed at my head. I remember stopping and wondering if I should get out of the room so the police could come in and deal with him, but I instead asked God, "What do I do?"

I heard God say, "You are staying!" So in that moment of time, I took two steps toward the man and the gun, not because I was brave, but because I wanted to do God's will and not chicken out. I stepped forward, ensuring I was in this to stay for the long haul.

Moving forward startled the man because he didn't expect that at all. He again yelled for me to get out, and my response was, "No, I'm staying here with you. I will not leave you until you have put the gun down and given up the idea of killing yourself."

The man began to tell me how God hated him and wanted him dead. I assured him of the opposite, that God loved him and that it was Satan that hated him and wanted him dead. After several minutes of dialog, he took the gun off the direction of my head and put his arms down.

I reached out and removed the gun from his hand and put it behind my back, just as the police decided to come in. There were two policemen by then, as the other police car had just arrived.

Upon finding us in the room together, the policemen let

me continue to talk with the man and eventually he calmed down even more and gave up the knife that the police noticed was in his side pocket.

They eventually took him in for evaluation and later I would get to relive those events through the eyes of three of the people I had contact with that night. I met with the man who wanted to die and his mother, and I also met with the policeman who sent me in.

The man who wanted to die that night said that he knew if he pointed a gun at the policeman he would get shot. He also said when I came around the corner, it was not part of his plan.

I shared with him what I already knew—God had a different plan and it was to save this man's life.

When I had spoken to his mom after all was done that night, she said that she couldn't get my name out of her head until she called me. Over and over she said she heard, "Call John, call John!" I told her God wanted her to call me.

The policeman had a bulletproof vest on and a gun that night when he sent me in. He said the reason he sent me in was that he had prayed to God to help him not shoot the man in the house when he got the call. The policeman said when he arrived at the home and saw me, he knew it was God who sent me so he sent me in.

The policeman apologized, but I assured him that it was the right thing to do since I had no gun and could not have taken a shot at the man. Even though I was only armed with the presence of God, it was enough for me.

To those of you thinking that the policeman was wrong, I understand. I also understand God had a plan to save a man who would surely have been killed that night. The policeman later on said he would have likely pulled the trigger as soon as he saw the gun. That would have been a perfectly normal response.

That night has meant a lot for me. It taught me how God is with you in troubled times and how His plans are so incredibly cool at times. I never once questioned why the police sent me in once I understood the outcome.

As history shows us from those who have gone before us, we can have a peace so incredible to the world that it becomes attractive for them and they will want it too. That can only come from living as God plans it for us, even to the point of a gun to our head.

God is good. All the time.

THE CHURCH

It has been said we are the arms and feet of Jesus. In other words, we are to do as he did on this earth and be like Him. When you look at the church today, what do you see? I am talking both in general and in your church.

From the book *Starving Jesus* by Craig Gross and J.R. Mahon, the following is said:

> Regardless of what his life looked like and how offensive his ministry was, Jesus continually told those around him to do two things: go and do. He healed people on the Sabbath. He was seen with prostitutes. He questioned authority. He ate with tax collectors, and he pulled lepers out the gutter. The first time he preached, people tried to kill him. Finally, he did the unthinkable. He gave himself willingly to die for a bunch of ragtag, ungrateful sinners. He needed everyone around him to understand the value of love, which is action in other people's lives.

When we look at Jesus' life, we that he was out there doing stuff to help others in ways we rarely see today, yet we are called to walk as Jesus walked.

In *Starving Jesus*, we see examples of things we should be doing. Here is the list: Give to the poor. Feed the hungry. Evangelize on a city street. Help a kid who has cancer. Join the fight against pornography. Share some time with the elderly. Love your neighbor. Play with and teach a little kid.

Make yourself available to a teenager who needs a mentor. Fix someone's car. Paint a house. Talk to a homosexual about his or her faith. Pull a drunk out of the gutter and give him something to eat. Give the homeless guy a place to crash. Bring a hooker to church. Spend the afternoon talking to an inmate at the local jail.

If this is not the church today, then why isn't it? Let's break it down to your life. Look at the list above and ask yourself if you are willing to do those things.

We are the church, and we need to get back to the business of doing what God asked us to do 2000 years ago—living out each day for Him and knowing He will be with us on the entire journey.

When the church decides to just meet together on Sunday mornings and do little else either individually or corporately, then the church is no longer a useful arm to Jesus. How can God have us help someone down and out if the arm doesn't work that will reach out and help that person get back up on their feet?

I remember an elder from another church asked if our church would help organize the collecting of clothes and other necessities for a family who had just lost their home in a fire. I asked why he was asking our church. I knew his church could also do it instead of asking ours to head it up.

His answer challenged me even more to live for Christ. He said: Your church is known for helping others and going out of your way to make sure things get done and to take care of those needs quickly. You do well at this type of thing.

Think about that. Another church asked us to do a task because they saw we were equipped to do it. On a different occasion another church in town asked me to organize a "vote yes for life" campaign. It was to encourage protecting life in our next election. That church was known for taking a stand for life and wanted other churches to help, so they asked me to ask all four of the local churches to participate. All said yes and each took one quarter of the town to walk door to door for this task.

One church saw how one could do it better. Another church who was good at a certain task wanted others to step up and do what they were already doing, so they passed the ministry on to another church to lead. Both were wise choices and we worked together as one on both of those tasks.

We are the church and God is ready to use us to let the world know that Jesus is the way, the truth, and the life. We can do better, and even in writing this page today, I am thinking of what part I can play in doing a better job of serving my Lord. Let's get back to the business of walking as Jesus walked. For that is the example we were given as to how to live a life pleasing to the Father.

You are the light of the world. A city set on a hill cannot be hidden. Nor do people light a lamp and put it under a basket, but on a stand, and it gives light to all in the house. In the same way, let your light shine before others, so that they may see your good works and give glory to your Father who is in heaven (Matthew 5:14-16).

Dear children, let us not love with words or speech but with actions and in truth (1 John 3:18).

KNOWING GOD

How well do you know God? At times it seems like I know God well, and then He teaches me how little I truly know of Him and yet I can see how much I need Him.

When we look in a mirror, we see a reflection of ourselves. It is like that with God, only the reflection we see is through glasses that are not correctly prescribed for us. It is like getting a glimpse of God but not getting to know Him fully.

If you were to build a relationship by conversations on phone calls with someone you never met in person, your view of them would be skewed. You would not know what they looked like, nor would you see the facial expressions and hand gestures they use when speaking. You would not know them nearly as much as if you had been with them face to face.

Yes, you could attempt to describe things about God, just like scripture describes God, but to know Him fully would mean you would need to be with Him. And if you are reading this today, then you are not with Him face to face. To be with Him is away from this life and body and to be present with Him.

Every day I can know God better and every day I can understand His will for my life more fully, but to know God fully for who He is will have to wait till I go home to be with Him.

Think about it. He made the heavens and the earth. He created us out of dust and made us in His image. He has a plan for each one of us, and it is a good plan. He has shown us the beauty of His creation and the awe of a baby being born.

God has given us His Word so that we might know Him and His Son, and so that we might know how to live, yet do you really know God well? His Word says if we draw near to God, He will draw hear to us. It says, "be still and know that I am God." So He clearly says we can have a relationship with Him and know Him, yet there are limits in this life to how well we know Him.

Think about someone you admire. It may be a sports star, teacher, or an author you love to read. It may be your spouse or your pastor. Whoever it is, no matter how much you have seen them or listened to them speak or read what they have written, you will not know everything about them.

You could live with your spouse for 50 years, and you will know a lot about them but not everything. We are not able to see God as He is yet. We will when we stand before Him, and every knee will bow and everyone will confess Jesus is Lord. At that point we will see God for who He is.

What God has shown me is that He loves me very much, so much so that He came up with a plan for my life and has shown me it is better than my plan. He has come to my aid and saved me from eternity away from Him. He has never failed me and has never given up on me.

When I am close to Him, there is no fear of anything and I have a hope and a future worth living. He builds my faith up as I serve others and leads me to better things. And every day I know Him better than the day before, so I strive to grow in the knowledge of the One who created me. For He is worthy of my praise and of my life that is given fully to Him.

Paul wrote about knowing God in the following passage.

> *For now we see only a reflection as in a mirror; then we shall see face to face. Now I know in part; then I shall know fully, even as I am fully known. And now these three remain: faith, hope and love. But the greatest of these is love* (1 Corinthians 13:12-13).

I know God enough to know I want to know Him better to do His will and experience the joy and peace He promises to those who love Him. I long to walk as Jesus walked and to know God is with me and that He will encourage me along life journey.

Even if life becomes what seems to be unbearable, I have been shown that it is still bearable if God is with me. For I can make it through all things if I have God helping me get through every minute of every day.

I may not know God fully yet, but I do know God!

GOD LOVES HUMOR

Genesis 1:27 says we were created in God's image, and from that passage we can see if man has a built-in sense of humor then so does God. As we live and experience laughter with a sense of peace and joy, then we can understand that God also enjoys those things too.

Scripture has times of irony, sarcasm, happiness, laughter, and joy that come from God Himself, through His Son Jesus and through His Word.

Proverbs 17:22 says, "A joyful heart is good medicine, but a crushed spirit dries up the bones."

In 1 Samuel 5:1-5 we can see God's sense of humor. The Philistines had captured the Ark of the Covenant and placed it in the temple of their god Dagon, and they later found their idol fallen face down in front of the Ark. They came in and put the statue back up, and God once again knocked it down and broke its head off.

Luke 6:41 says why do you look at the sliver that is in your brother's eye, but you do not perceive the beam that is in your own eye?

During my lifetime there has been much humor in some very dangerous places, and it has been apparent that when we are close to God there is no fear. I was filled with only joy. With that joy came with it peace that we would indeed make it as long as God was with us.

Here are two examples. A friend and I were in Nepal driving down the road in the Himalayan mountain passes with a drop off of thousands of feet and no guard rails. We could see that there were many vehicles that had gone over it as we looked out over the side of the mountain.

I would film the drives, while my friend was in the back. He asked why I liked the front, so I said: "When we go over the cliff and die, I will get to see Jesus first." He laughed and replied, "Only part of a second sooner." Again we laughed about what we were encountering that was so different from home in America.

Another time we were standing in the middle of a road with two lanes of traffic on both sides of us with one foot of space between the traffic to stand on. I got hit by the mirror of a car and we could all see this could end badly if we didn't get across soon.

I began to sing, "I surrender all. All to Jesus, I surrender, I surrender all." He again laughed and said, "How can you sing at a time like this?" It was because I had God with me, and we were able to enjoy our time in Nepal in spite of what looked like craziness going on around us.

I have since gone back to Nepal again to enjoy this beautiful place and would love to again and again and again. Even though we can be placed by God where there is intense trouble, we can still find humor in the situation because with God, all things are possible and nothing is too big for Him.

In places that look terrifying to the world, it is possible to find joy and be able to encourage your brother or sister in the Lord. God expects us to be able to give Him our lives and trust in Him to be faithful to us. God never fails.

In Thessalonians we can see that the church was and is to be encouraging. We are to live a life not only pleasing to God but a life that encourages one another.

Therefore encourage one another and build each other up, just as in fact you are doing (1 Thessalonians 5:11).

I will end this section with the most surprising time I have ever burst into laughter. A group of believers were gathered with a man who was oppressed by demons. We had prayed for some time and many had left the man, but there was one who was not leaving as quickly as the others did.

As we prayed, the demon spoke out loud through the man. He said he was not going to go no matter how hard we prayed. Then it added, "For I am like God!"

At that point God removed everything left that was evil in this man and the demon was gone in one second. There was total silence in the room and the man was completely free in that instant.

We started laughing at the fact God had listened to this demon say he was like God, and it was as if God said "Enough of this nonsense" and it was instantly over. No fight, no struggle, no more anything.

We were in awe of God and laughed at how easy it was for God to do this for the man. It built our faith in God and encouraged us to continue to help others receive freedom that only God can give.

I even remember someone asking, "Should we be laughing right now?" The answer was yes we should because we were made in God's image, and He indeed has a wonderful sense of humor.

WHEN LOVE IS GONE

In February 2013 I awoke from an incredible dream. I was shaking and trying desperately to figure out what had just happened. Was it a dream or was I actually there? It was that real and so very terrifying.

I got up and immediately began to cry out to God that He would never let that happen to me again. Throughout the entire day it was all I could think about. In the end it was evident that the story of that dream had to be passed on to others to hear. So here is what happened.

In the dream I found myself in a room that was like a prison cell. After sitting alone for a while, it dawned on me that I was truly alone—no family, no guards, no one. It was awful and it was not a place I wanted to be.

I cried out for help and at first nothing happened, but then I realized something. I recognized that even in this dark place God was with me and that gave me comfort, yet I was still alone in the cell with no hope in sight. God let me sit and wonder what was going to happen to me, when would help come, if ever. It was the loneliest place I had ever been.

Then something much worse happened. God Himself left me and I was now separated from God. It was like hell to me. To have love leave and be left without hope was terrifying. I cried out like never before and there was no answer. My cries became screams and still no answer.

The time in that cell went on for what felt like forever, and the separation from God was worse than any other bad experience I had ever had. To be separated from God was overwhelming and there was no peace and no joy. As I sat there wondering how long I would have to endure this agony, God came back. He said to remember what He had shown me and tell others, which is what I am doing today. I'm telling you who are reading this that separation from God is not something to be taken lightly.

Trying to explain this experience is not easy and in attempting to help you feel what I did, I would ask you to think of the following.

If you lost all your family in a car wreck, lost all your possessions, friends, job, your home, and had nothing left to live for, how would you feel? Well, even in that state of mind, it would be nothing in comparison to having to experience an eternal separation from God. On a scale of bad, I would say a million times worse and even worse than that.

I pray that I will never again experience that and yet my love for God actually grew from that experience because I realized that sometimes I take having the Holy Spirit with me for granted. I have not been to hell and do not wish to, but I can tell you the hell I experienced that day was real and terrifying, and it changed me. My appreciation for God is greater and my love for Him has grown from that day forward.

God is Love and because of that fact, we can rest in Him and know He is better than anything else we could ever have. He is perfect peace and He will never fail us, for God is Love.

The LORD your God is in your midst, a mighty one who will save; he will rejoice over you with gladness; he will quiet you by his love; he will exult over you with loud singing (Zephaniah 3:17).

I love those who love me, and those who seek me diligently find me (Proverbs 8:17).

My hope for you this day is that you will not take having God in your life for granted and for those of you who don't yet know God, that He is waiting for you to want Him. He loves you very much and the following verse sums up His love for you very much.

For God so loved the world, that he gave his only Son, that whoever believes in him should not perish but have eternal life (John 3:16).

MY BIRTHDAY

In 2013 on my birthday, I was heading home from work to have a relaxing night with my family. My son Jacob and his friend Denver had told me that they were going to celebrate my birthday by frying up some fish they had caught at the Missouri River just down the road from us.

Upon arriving home I got out of my truck, headed into the back door of my home, and walked in to utter and total chaos. Grease and flour were everywhere. M kids were all trying to tell me what had happened at the same time.

My wife had left the house upset, telling the kids she wasn't coming back. The homeless man who had been living with us for about a month left too. He left because of what had just happened and knew his part in it all.

As the voices finally lowered, one of my kids defended the other brother, and my oldest tried to explain what he knew of what had just happened. My mind was trying to take all the information in and figure out how to respond to it.

After examining the situation, I left the house to find my wife. She had walked to a park nearby and was sitting at a picnic table. I helped her work through some of the problems that had happened with the homeless man and the oil and flour being thrown everywhere, and she headed for home.

Next I was off to find the former homeless man. I found him a half hour later and began to walk and talk with him. After an hour or more he too said he would come back to the house and apologize for his part in the matter. God had sent this man to my family to live with us, and he would eventually get back on his feet and move on to a life where he was able to work though things much better than before.

As the night unfolded, it became apparent that all would end well and everyone would move to a place of better understanding of each other as the days moved forward.

After everyone went off to bed, I headed to the prayer room. I was a bit taken back by all that had happened, but I never once got excited or angry or frustrated. My question to God was why was I able to have a sound mind and think clearly in the midst of all of the chaos around me?

I had experienced a good day with the Lord and went home from work to a total zoo. Yet through all of it, I had a sound mind, the ability to love, and was able to know what to do.

Then a verse came to mind 2 Timothy 1:7, "For God gave us a spirit not of fear but of power and love and self-control."

I saw there in that verse that God promises us self-control and the power to get through what lies before us and also the ability to love the unlovable. That verse summed up my day with God. He gave that to me and it was evident as I prayed.

God showed me that we are an instrument that He uses for His glory and honor and praise. I was so thankful for the opportunity to learn that lesson. Even today my family talks about that day and says they wish it all wouldn't have happened on my birthday. My answer is always the same. I wouldn't have changed a thing.

PS. You are probably wondering about the oil and flour. Well, the oil got spilled when my son carried the fryer that was full of oil into the house and it fell through the bottom of the box. The man living with us took a 10 lb. bag of flour and threw it all over the oil and everything else, trying to help.

The other events just rolled off the first until everyone was upset with everything that had just transpired. We laugh now about that day, as best we can, but that lesson was worth the struggle and helped me see how God was changing me from the inside out.

CAN I CALL YOU DAD?

Over the years we have had many people come into our home to live with us. It might be just for a week but with others it was for a year or more. All have different struggles, as do we all. Yet several even came to a place where they began to call me Dad. I would like to share about one of those young men and tell you some of his story.

In July 2013 I got a call from a friend in Texas who had taken a homeless man to live with him and his family. "John, we are having trouble handling him and thought of you and wondered if you could take him in with you."

Ha-ha I thought. What a wonderful invitation for me to take. I had taken in quite a few people by then and my wife reminded me that it wasn't good to not work together on deciding who we should take into our home. So I turned to her and said, "You decide this one."

The following day God began to speak to Jill and as she did her devotions, He moved her heart toward taking this man into our home and so she made her decision. I went and got him in Omaha and then headed home with our new guest who lived with us for almost a year.

He had been homeless as of the previous month or so. He was a member of two different gangs growing up and was in and out of foster homes. He spent two tours in the Marines in Afghanistan. His wife had divorced him. He was a mess and had never truly understood the concept of love, not the love God has anyway. In his world if you stole something for your gang, you got love through a reward. If he fought hard enough, he would get respect and felt that was love, yet he never truly understood love.

We taught him how to do his own laundry and his dirty dishes. He had no paperwork, so for six months we worked step by step to get his military discharge papers, a social security card, his birth certificate, and so forth.

As time went on, he began to change and understand how God loved him and so did we. Many days he would storm out of the house angry only to return and work through the event that caused him grief. Something special happened.

During his angry times he would say, "Don't ever think about me ever calling you Dad." I had never asked that of him, but he saw others call me Dad and just wanted to set the record straight that he was not going to ever do that.

Months went by, and one day he wanted to meet with me so he could ask me something important. He looked very serious, so we went into my prayer room to be alone to talk. There he shared how much he had grown close to God as he lived with us and wanted to make a special request.

I agreed to it, not knowing what he was going to ask. He said, "Can I call you Dad?" "Certainly you can," was my reply. "I would like that very much, son." He said I was more like a father to him than his own father, and that I was very important to him in drawing closer to God.

This man today is still a part of my life. Even though he lives several states away, we talk on the phone, text, and message each other quite often. This man is precious to me and my family, and we are very grateful that he came into our lives and became a part of it, and so gained another son, who calls me Dad.

I would like to end this section with a question. Could you ever take a stranger into your home and let him live with you for a year? The following verses are to encourage us. We are to be the hands and feet of Jesus in this broken world.

When the Son of Man comes in his glory, and all the angels with him, he will sit on his glorious throne. All the nations will be gathered before him, and he will separate the people one from another as a shepherd separates the sheep from the goats. He will put the sheep on his right and the goats on his left.

Then the King will say to those on his right, "Come, you who are blessed by my Father; take your inheritance, the kingdom prepared for you since the creation of the world. For I was hungry and you gave me something to eat, I was thirsty and you gave me something to drink, I was a stranger and you invited me in, I needed clothes and you clothed me, I was sick and you looked after me, I was in prison and you came to visit me."

Then the righteous will answer him, "Lord, when did we see you hungry and feed you, or thirsty and give you something to drink? When did we see you a stranger and invite you in, or needing clothes and clothe you? When did we see you sick or in prison and go to visit you?" The King will reply, "Truly I tell you, whatever you did for one of the least of these brothers and sisters of mine, you did for me" (Matthew 25:31-40).

GOD IS GOOD, ALWAYS

As I was reading some of the stories I had written in my journal, a few jumped out of the pages at me. They were showing me how God's plans are so very good. God showed me that choices I had made to follow Him have had results I could not have known at the time that would turn out to be so incredible.

After speaking at a conference, God told me that the reason I was able to witness to many people and say they were going to move out of their comfort zones was that we had taken in a homeless man into our lives for almost a year.

He also said seeing Yami's family all come to know the Lord wouldn't have been spoken of at the conference if I hadn't listened to God last year and invited this woman into our home. Later that year all her family came to know Jesus.

After speaking about my trip to Nepal at Gettysburg High School, again I was reminded that when I listened to God, He gave me opportunities to serve Him in ways others haven't had the privilege of doing.

And God showed me how having a gun put to my head caused my faith to grow, not shrink. His plans are always best.

There is no real easy way to explain it. My walk with God would not be the same without the experiences that I have had of following Him wherever He leads me. I have been in dark places and yet the light coming from me (Jesus Light) expelled the darkness.

Following God's instructions and driving to a certain spot caused me to help stop someone from suicide. Going to a home when I felt God's nudge gave me a chance to help a family in need.

Setting aside a room for God, as He asked me to do, has given me a place to seek Him, to cry before Him, to hear from Him, and to receive a blessing by just walking in the room with a heart wanting to be with Him and Him alone.

Putting a cross in my yard helped me understand more fully what it is like to take a stand for God in a way others will not do. I have been called a Jesus freak for the life I live in Christ, and yet it has been good.

To be accused of standing for Jesus in everything we do will cause others to question what we are doing, but it will lend itself to opportunities to talk about the Jesus I love so dearly.

I do not have days where the opportunities are not there. I can say that God always has something for me. Every day there is another call, or verse to read, or prayer to be sent God's way, or another breath to breathe that will cause me to recognize just who gave me that breath, for God is good and what He gives us is good always.

And we know that God causes all things to work together for good to those who love God, to those who are called according to His purpose (Romans 8:28).

SPIRITUAL WARFARE

Of Zebulun 50,000 seasoned troops, equipped for battle with all the weapons of war, to help David with single-ness of purpose (1 Chronicles 12:33).

For our struggle is not against flesh and blood, but against the rulers, against the authorities, against the powers of this dark world and against the spiritual forces of evil in the heavenly realms (Ephesian 6:12).

Experienced soldiers prepare for battle with every type of weapon to help their cause with absolute and total loyalty. When we look at Ephesian 6:12 and begin to think about what that means to us who not only recognize the battle but fight in those battles that we face, it changes what we must do to be ready for it.

Spiritual warfare is a ministry people don't want to get involved in because they know it is serious. This ministry draws the line—you are either close to God or you had better stay away from these battles that set people free. When you are truly with God in this battle, you will fight and destroy the enemy.

"Teacher," said John, "we saw someone driving out demons in your name and we told him to stop, because he was not one of us." "Do not stop him," Jesus said. "For no one who does a miracle in my name can in the next moment say anything bad about me, for whoever is not against us is for us" (Mark 9:38-40).

Christians dealing with the fight against spiritual darkness will stay very close to God because they know there is no hope without Christ in the battle between good and evil.

Those who fight this battle head on have some things in common. They tend to pray more, fast more, study more, and have more compassion for those who are involved in these struggles. Their worship of God seems to become even more passionate, and these battles develop perseverance and increase stamina. When you fight in these battles, you walk with God, learn discernment, and speak the Word of God, which teaches you to exercise the authority and power of Jesus Christ.

To win these battles it takes all you have learned about God and more. It takes faith to stand and fight a battle that you cannot totally understand. God will teach you how to fight and will calm your heartbeats that you will not panic about the situation. The Holy Spirit is there with you leading you along the way.

My closeness to God was noticeable to others immediately when I joined in on the fight against the enemy in spiritual warfare. They said something was different about my walk with the Lord. They saw I was stronger and seemed more on fire for the One who made me and told me so.

Those who didn't understand these battles did come around to a better understanding eventually. When you are producing fruit and loving the Lord with all your heart, soul, mind, and strength, it is noticed.

When you stand for truth in these battles and come out on top, then your faith is increased even more. When the enemy has trembled and fled, you realize the truth of the scripture that says we will do as Christ did.

Scripture says we will walk as Jesus walked and do what He did, but few of us experience the total package of what Christ did as an example for us to follow. Today as I write this section, I am here to say Paul was correct when he said we fight not against flesh and blood but against principalities of darkness.

We are all in the battle, but most don't see it. When God's Word says capture your thoughts, it is because there are thoughts that are not yours bombarding you that are evil. Scripture wouldn't say that if it were not so. The battle starts in your mind. The thoughts come, you entertain them, and then they can turn eventually into action.

Those choices can cause the enemy to get a foothold into your life, which can turn into a stronghold and eventually into a stranglehold. We need to stop the attack when it first starts and flee from it.

It is by the name of Jesus that we have victory, and it is by His name we pray. When you have those thoughts, cast them aside in the name of Jesus. Your journey will become better and the attack will stop there.

The enemy is real. In John 10:10 it says: "The thief comes only to steal and kill and destroy; I have come that they may have life, and have it to the full."

In that passage you see how Satan wants to steal, destroy your life, and kill you. You can also see that Jesus came to give us a life that is complete in Him.

What a stark difference! We have an enemy that wants us dead and a God who wants to give us life, and not just any life but a full life with God that is worth living.

Jesus offers us His light and teaches us what it means to live for Him through the Holy Spirit living in us. I chose

Christ and live for Him. He has never failed me, nor forsaken me and is always there for me. Jesus sits at the right hand of the Father speaking on my behalf and is speaking on your behalf.

My prayer for you:

Thank You, Jesus, for the victories you give us every day, because of Your victory on the cross. Help us to recognize the fight is before us and just how real it is. We love You, Lord, and look forward to all You have for us. Help us to stand and fight for You and be instruments for You, oh Lord. In Jesus' name I pray. Amen.

GOD IS IN CONTROL

God being in control of all things is a concept to some people that causes them doubts about Him. I have talked to many of those who do not believe in either God or that He is control of all things. I know it is a struggle for many, but for me I have seen His control in action, sometimes unexpectedly.

A verse that has helped me understand how things work is Romans 8:28.

And we know that in all things God works for the good of those who love him, who have been called according to his purpose.

I have had many bad things happen to me, and as I reflect on them, I am reminded of the sovereignty of God. I have been drawn to Him in those times, and He has been faithful. I am a walking example of someone who should not be here today.

Think about the worst day of your life and if you are a believer, you will likely know that God was there with you. In my darkest hours He has been there, and the closest times of my life with God were when my worst tragedies took place.

When life is good and all the bills are paid, most of us are not looking for God; but we turn often to Him when we are struggling and don't have the answer to life's question ourselves. Only then do we recognize our need of Him.

Many are the plans in the mind of a man, but it is the purpose of the Lord that will stand (Proverbs 19:21).

In this verse God says His purpose will stand. So what He wants, He will get. I have seen that play out myself many times.

I know someone who was dying and had no hope from the doctors. This person was told life would end soon. When we asked God to step in on their behalf and heal them, He chose to heal them.

Another man with inoperable brain cancer too was healed in an instant, yet others are not healed. Why? God doesn't always work through healing. Sometimes He shows Himself through dying. When you see proof of peace at the end of life and a person goes from this life to the next with a smile on their face, it is a testimony as to how God is in control.

He knows our thoughts, our actions, and He knows what is best for us. Some days will be harder than others, and one day will end up being our last, yet God is in control of all our lives if we let Him.

Even those who do not choose God are living examples of God's control. He is allowing them to live even as they deny His very existence.

An extreme example of His control that I witnessed was absolutely astounding at the time for those of us who watched God at work. We were on a prayer walk and a dog began to growl and bark uncontrollably at us.

We turned to the dog and began to pray, knowing the dog wanted to attack us. Two of us asked God to stop the dog right then and there in Jesus' name. As soon as we proclaimed His name, the dog stopped growling and lay down on the ground. The dog began to place its paws over its head and whimper. When we were done praying, we were able to walk up to the dog and pet it. This dog became completely calm because God decided to control that dog. We didn't do anything but ask in Jesus' name for God to control that dog and He did.

Many other times you have probably prayed and God answered, stepped in on your behalf, saved you from disaster, and you didn't even know it. I know He has time and time again throughout history stepped in to save us.

Look at our world now. If the earth wasn't made the way God intended it, we would not exist. If our bodies weren't made the way they are, we would not have life. We do not have to look far to see God's handiwork and how it all comes together to make this world a place in which we can experience life and eventually death.

Believe me when I say that I am in the Father and the Father is in me; or at least believe on the evidence of the works themselves. Very truly I tell you, whoever believes in me will do the works I have been doing, and they will do even greater things than these, because I am going to the Father. And I will do whatever you ask in my name, so that the Father may be glorified in the Son. You may ask me for anything in my name, and I will do it (John 14:11-14).

Doesn't this passage about sum it up for us? God will do as we ask, whatever it is, if we asking according to His will at the time. Until the day I die, I know that God can and still does all things, and nothing can stop Him from doing whatever He wishes to do.

The LORD does whatever pleases him, in the heavens and on the earth, in the seas and all their depths (Psalm 135:6).

HE WILL SUPPLY YOUR NEEDS

The following are miracles on how God supplies our every need, even when there seemed to be no hope, and yet God was there to take care of all those needs.

In the years 2012-13 my family was blessed to see many miracles. When I needed rest, God provided for it. There were times we were invited to people's homes and were blessed with a refreshing night of encouragement.

When I went to Africa in 2012, financially I had no way of paying for that trip. When God began calling me to places, I asked God to provide the funds so that I would not have to go fundraising for those trips. I asked that He would supply for my every need. I didn't know if it would be through my business or through others, but I knew He heard my prayer.

That trip cost thousands of dollars, as did our trip to Thailand. We also purchased my parent's share of the store during that time, and God had us take in a homeless man for almost a year. We also paid for several trips for people to see their loved ones because they didn't have the means to do so.

We took in two more young people from Texas in the summer of 2013, right after our friend Steven moved out. My daughter's tuition at college was over $11,000 for our share in 2012. I also made four trips to Texas to work with the two churches we care for so very much. My new car was purchased in December 2012 and the list goes on and on. The following is how God took care of us.

When I was going to Africa, people out of nowhere sent us money. All I had done was tell some friends I was making the trip and put it on my Facebook page asking for prayer, as the plans were being made for this trip. Checks began to pour in from people all over the country, telling me they were led by God to do this for me. When all was done, everything was completely paid for. God supplied all my needs.

When we went to Thailand, we had saved up enough for Jill and I to go, but not the missionary's daughter we were taking with us. Again the money came in right before we were to leave.

When I was given the opportunity to speak at our church, a couple gave me $1000 for the trips to Texas. That money paid for three of those trips. When it came down to buying the store, the purchase amount matched what God wanted me to pay, and I never mentioned the amount to my parents.

In less than a year I have put 25,000 miles on our new car. That car came two years after giving the jeep to my son and driving my old pickup, which I still drive every day to work.

I have not had to run up a credit card debt and have been able to pay every time a need has arisen. There have been times a bill was due and the same day, the money showed up.

On Thanksgiving 2013 God nudged me to ask one of my children's friends from South Korea, who goes to Moody Bible Institute, what he was doing for Thanksgiving. He said sitting in his dorm room with no place to go, so I asked him about Christmas, and he said he would probably be doing the same thing.

I mentioned him coming here and he said: "You can't bring me there. It's like 14 hours driving, how so? Ha-ha, that would be awesome though and thanks for asking ha-ha."

He didn't think I was serious. I told him I meant it when I said I was thinking about bringing him to our home for Christmas and he said the following: "Wow, seriously what a thankful thing that there is someone who would actually take care of me."

A couple days later my best friend came to the store for coffee and asked how Thanksgiving dinner at the church went and in our discussion I told him about our friend from South Korea.

At that point, out of the blue, my friend said he would like to pay for half the ticket. This is a man who by no means is wealthy yet was wanting to help supply the needs of another. I said I would wait to see if that was necessary. A week went by and someone from another town gave me the money to cover the ticket. The man said he felt God wanted him to do that for me and my wife. I am so blessed to have such friends who care about others above their own needs.

I have come to find out God's Word is right on when it says: "And my God will supply all your needs according to His riches in glory in Christ Jesus" (Philippians 4:19).

HOPE

Hope is anticipating something good in the future. Our hope as believers is on the kingdom of God. I have read many books about people who ended up being martyrs for Jesus. Many stories have what seems like a bad ending to a life filled with hope in Christ.

As I study these situations, there is something that seems to be consistent—they have peace in these terrible times. You have to wonder why. How is it possible to have peace when you and your entire family are going to be executed for being a follower of Jesus?

A family was forced to dig their own graves and step in the hole and wait to be shot, when one child bolted into the woods to escape. His father called out to his son and asked why he would choose to live a while longer on this earth when he would be in eternity with his family in heaven in a few moments.

His son came out and the family was executed together. How could this happen? Why would the son come out instead of running away from death that day? It is the hope we have in Christ. We have assurance in His death on the cross and His resurrection. They had something that was unique to those following Christ—perfect peace. The anticipation that there was something better than this life was real. They believed it was better to die for Christ than to live.

Another story that sticks out in my mind is that of Horatio G. Spafford who wrote the song "It Is Well With

My Soul." The song is one of thanksgiving and praise to God in the midst of terrible loss and circumstances that seem almost too much to bear.

Horatio was a Chicago lawyer who had become quite wealthy and lost most all of it in a Chicago fire after the loss of their four year old son. When his wife and four daughters sailed to Europe ahead of him, Horatio received a telegram from his wife, Anna, which read, "Saved alone."

Their ship had collided with another vessel and sank, and his four daughters had all been lost with his wife the only survivor from his family.

Horatio boarded the next ship out of New York to go to Anna. As they sailed, the captain called Horatio to the ship's bridge and shared with him the spot where his daughters had perished. Horatio then returned to his cabin and wrote "It Is Well With My Soul."

It Is Well With My Soul
When peace, like a river, attendeth my way,
When sorrows like sea billows roll;
Whatever my lot, Thou has taught me to say,
It is well, it is well, with my soul.
Though Satan should buffet, though trials should come,
Let this blest assurance control,
That Christ has regarded my helpless estate,
And hath shed His own blood for my soul.
My sin, oh, the bliss of this glorious thought!
My sin, not in part but the whole,
Is nailed to the cross, and I bear it no more,
Praise the Lord, praise the Lord, O my soul!
For me, be it Christ, be it Christ hence to live:

If Jordan above me shall roll,
No pang shall be mine, for in death as in life
Thou wilt whisper Thy peace to my soul.
But, Lord, 'tis for Thee, for Thy coming we wait,
The sky, not the grave, is our goal;
Oh, trump of the angel! Oh, voice of the Lord!
Blessed hope, blessed rest of my soul!
And Lord, haste the day when my faith shall be sight,
The clouds be rolled back as a scroll;
The trump shall resound, and the Lord shall descend,
Even so, it is well with my soul.

Through Him we have also obtained access by faith into this grace in which we stand, and we rejoice in the hope of the glory of God. More than that, we rejoice in our sufferings, knowing that suffering produces endurance, and endurance produces character, and character produces hope, and hope does not put us to shame, because God's love has been poured into our hearts through the Holy Spirit who has been given to us.

GOD KNOWS THE FUTURE

Have you ever wondered about the future? I have, and often think about what plans God has for me in the years to come. Scripture says worry about today for tomorrow will worry about itself.

I have had a few things happen where God showed me the future, and other times He showed me how He was looking out for me before I was even aware of the problem that was coming. Here are a few examples of God's provision of knowledge when He wants to show us something.

Before going to Africa, I had two dreams where I saw a woman smiling at me and asking me for something, and another dream where I was on my knees playing with children. I was high fiving them and shaking their hands. I didn't think much of the dreams at the time and kind of put them aside.

While in Africa those two dreams came true, and the people in them were the exact people in the dream. God had shown me what was to come and I wasn't expecting it. Imagine what I thought when it happened unexpectedly like that!

On January 19, 2013 I had another crazy thing happen. I saw a basketball game played where my favorite team, Duke, was beaten handily by Miami, although I knew Duke was ranked No. 1. I even knew the final score. It was a vision so real that I thought I actually saw it as it was played out in real time.

Four days later, my son Jacob and I were in Mitchell,

South Dakota, at a restaurant and a basketball game was playing on the TV. It was the same game I saw played out a few days earlier in my vision. I said to my son, "Why is there a game that has already been played being shown in prime-time tonight?"

Jacob said, "Dad, that game is live." I said, "No, it isn't. I know the final score is 90-63, and that it was a crushing defeat for Duke by the Hurricanes." He just stared at me and with about half the game to go, we ate and watched the game play out at that restaurant. The final score was 90-63! As the Hurricanes ran on the floor and celebrated, my son just stared at the TV screen.

In the end I found out it truly was a live game and that what I originally saw was a vision or dream that God gave me days before to prepare me to accept future things He would eventually show me later. That moment gave me much more faith that God knows our future and has the best plan for us.

In March 2015 I went back to Nepal with four others to see what God was doing and to encourage our friends working there in the medical field. On our there, we encountered a plane ticket problem that would cost us an extra $2000, and we didn't have the extra money to cover that cost. We had to use a credit card and at that moment, I asked God to cover the amount for us. Not wanting debt and knowing He has other plans for me, it seemed like a fair request to ask.

After the trip, I arrived home on a Saturday night, visited with my family, and went off to bed. The next morning I went to early morning prayer time at our church. After we finished, I went to my family's mailbox and found a card with a check in it. The card said that before we left for Nepal, God told her and her husband to give me an exact amount of money—$2000. As I looked at the check, it was for that amount. My tears began to flow and I wept out loud to the point where a friend came and put his hand on my shoulder.

God knew we would come up short on that trip. He knew it would be difficult for me to find the money for that extra expense. He prodded a couple to give before the event even happened. Imagine that in your life! God knows what you are going to go through and would actually take care of the problem before you know it even exists.

When I see how God provides, it builds my faith in Him and in the plan He has for me. It gives me the courage to do the impossible. Many times I am unqualified for what God has for me to do, yet He never fails. He is always providing what I need to finish the task He gives me.

Scripture predicted Jesus' coming, His death, and the victory He would have over death. God told us in His Word about the end of the world as we know it. He has told us about the trouble we will have in this life. Time after time his predictions have come true, every single one.

He knows everything about every day we live and has those days numbered. So since He knows all things and has the best plan for you, I would encourage you who are believers today to seek God for wisdom, knowledge, and the strength to do His will.

If you do not know God, then let me encourage you to seek God out and let Him have your life today so that you can have a better plan than you have now—a plan made by the One who made you.

CAN GOD SPEAK DIRECTLY TO YOU?

One of the most asked questions I get is: "How does God speak to you, John?" The second is, "Do you think God would speak to me?"

The answer to the first is God speaks through His Word (the Bible), He speaks through others, and He speaks through prayer. Yet the question asked almost always is, "How does God speak directly to you?"

It has taken me years to get to the point where the conversations flow freely at times with our heavenly Father. Yet seldom does God choose to communicate this way with me.

When people hear my stories, they will undoubtedly say it is something they also wish to experience. I let them know it is something that they do not have to wait years to achieve. God wishes to speak to all who love Him.

When God speaks directly to me, it is with authority and truth. He doesn't lie and what He says will happen. I am corrected by Him and challenged also. He sometimes uses humor and sometimes gives me clear direction or warning of what is to come.

One month I had three men come to me asking how they could hear God. Each person was unique and each one did hear God's voice clearly.

The first asked me for advice on listening for and hearing God's voice. I prayed that God would speak and He gave the man directly two instructions. He finished his conversation with me and went and did what God asked.

The second man doubted he could ever hear God again. He had done so before but not for some time. Again I prayed, and God let him know He heard him through reminding him of the verse he had just read that day: "Here I Am."

The third man, after talking to me about seeking God's voice, set out to hear God by fasting and asking God specific questions. At the end of the day, the man called me and said God told him He wouldn't answer the questions that he had asked. The man was upset that God didn't answer him, yet God did speak to him, but it just wasn't the answer for which he was looking.

Over the course of fifty years of my life, I have heard God speak many times, and sometimes He speaks with a wonderful sense of humor.

After returning home from Thailand and thinking of all the incredible and miraculous things God did while I was there, I heard God's voice.

God: "What are you thinking?"

John: "You outdid yourself in Thailand!"

God: "I cannot outdo Myself!"

John: "Okay, You are right; You cannot out do Yourself, but You can do more than I ever expected."

God: "I enjoy your company."

John: "Thank You, Father. I cherish these conversations very much."

God: "As do I, for I know your heart."

John: "Thank You, Father, for loving me so."

These are simple conversations that can encourage me to live for Him. Even with the fact that God speaks, I must let you know that it comes with a warning. The enemy will also speak to you. You will need to discern the difference. The enemy is sneaky and manipulative. His goal is to steal, destroy, and kill you. The enemy's words will not bring you closer to God but away from Him.

God can and does still speak directly to people, yet if you do not discern His voice, you will fall prey to the enemy. The best way I can describe knowing the difference is that it is learned.

If a mother was blindfolded and put in a room with a hundred different children crying out for their mothers, the mother would know the voice of her child and be able to hear the child's cries. It is the same with us. We can know the voice of God and decipher His voice from all the others that the enemy throws at us.

Another thing to know is His voice will not contradict His Word. The Bible is perfect, the best example we have of perfect instructions for our lives. I read it every single day. I also pray every single day.

Hearing God's voice has sent me to other countries and shown me things to come, yet time and time again I turn to His Word for directions on how to live. Seek God every day for His instructions and He will answer.

My sheep hear my voice, and I know them, and they follow me (John 10:27).

HIS PLAN

At this point most of you know that God has a plan for you, and it will not be a plan that we can fully think through and know all that is to come. God's Word says His thoughts are not our thoughts and His ways are not our ways so it should be apparent that we should not be shocked at what He tells us to do, whether it is from His Word or from God having others encourage us down a different path, or the Holy Spirit gently leading us to where we are to go.

One thing remains the same—God has a plan that is better for us, and if we follow Him, we will have success, maybe not the success we may be thinking of, but the success God has planned for our life.

God may ask you to lay down your life for another and allow you to be executed for the sake of the Cross. He may move you from your comfortable life to a life that will be a very hard one, which may not end the way you would have envisioned it. That does not mean it is not good. It does not mean it is not success. It means you did what God wanted and His plan was fulfilled.

God's plans are always best, and it has been proven to me thousands of times. God has sent me to a home to give all the money I had to someone and I did it. In that lesson I learned how God would continue to provide for me, without fail.

I have been on a plane that almost crashed, and God showed me that I had no fear of dying. Many times God has sent me to people's homes to pray or to make a phone call to encourage others; and if you asked them, they would tell you that at that moment it was God responding to their calls for help.

There are stories of martyred people who were burned alive and yet still singing praises to the Lord. That was a plan and that plan makes little sense to us, but it is the best plan. Moments like that can be used to show others the power of following the one, true God.

People have responded in history to those kinds of acts and been drawn to a relationship with God. A friend of mine told me a story of a missionary that she was working with who said she had never heard God speak to her before. One day as she was riding her scooter across town, God spoke to her.

God told her to go into the store next to her, head to the back, and spin around three times. First she questioned if it were God because she had not heard Him before. Then she thought it was too crazy so she started to leave, and again God said to go into the back of the store and spin around three times.

So she did. She went in and went to the back and quickly spun around three times and left in a hurry. As she was beginning to drive away, the owner, who had run out of the store, grabbed her arm and asked her, "Why did you do that?"

She said, "My God told me to do it." He said, "What God?" And her response was, "I am a follower of Jesus." He then proceeded to tell her that he was wondering if Jesus was really God as some had told him, so he said that he had just prayed: "Jesus, if you are real, then make one of Your followers come into my store, go to the back, and spin around three times." That day this man came to know the God who created the universe, the King of Kings and Lord of Lords, the Savior of the world, who is Jesus.

That man came to know God in part because the woman was faithful to the plan God had for her life. She did what God wanted her to do and it was a success. It was a good plan and it was the one that God wanted for her. It made no sense and certainly would not have been her plan, but it was the right thing to do at the right time to do it, and it produced fruit that will last forever because a man came to know God that day and gave his life to Him.

You see if you reasoned that one out, most people would not have done it. It makes no sense to go in a store and spin around three times, does it? But the plan was right, the plan was good, and that plan saved a man's life from eternal darkness that day.

"For my thoughts are not your thoughts, neither are your ways my ways," declares the Lord. "As the heavens are higher than the earth, so are my ways higher than your ways and my thoughts than your thoughts (Isaiah 55:8-9).

QUIET TIME

As I headed toward the beach in Oahu for my morning devotions, it seemed like any other day. The first words I heard after reaching the beach were from my Lord. He said, "It is going to be a very good day!"

I thought *I wonder what is in store for me today,* and indeed this day was different for God was going to teach me something that I wondered about for the past twenty years.

When God delivered me from all my addictions and made me new, He also told me about my future. Imagine being saved from death and having felt worthless just prior to that and then having God say to you that you are valuable to Him and are worth much more than you could ever imagine.

The day after handing God my life to use for His glory, God told me my future and some of what He said I would do in Jesus' name. I just could not understand how this was possible for a person like me.

I was still trying to understand how in an instant God changed me and then He said, "You, John, will do these things for Me."

It has been 20 years since He told me that, and now these things have been coming to pass in just the last three years.

The one question I had of all that He told me was, "Will I see it all happen?" You see, without telling you what it was He said, the things He told me would happen could occur during my lifetime, at my death, or after I die. I only know what is to come, not when it is to happen.

On January 20, 2014 on a beach in Waikiki, God told me the following: "I proclaim before you this day, John, that you will not die before seeing the fruit of your labor fulfilled in the manner I have given you."

I will get to see what was promised, and I can rest on His promises, for God never fails me, He never lies to me, He always does what He says and is faithful and true. That morning God also said it was going to be a great day and to stay near to Him and He would stay near to me. And so it was on that special day, as I stayed near to Him.

As we traveled the island, we saw many God-filled moments. An elderly man from China said to my friend Pastor Mark Teves that he knew a man who was a Christian decades ago that knew God. He told Mark that he came back to Hawaii to find God for himself. Mark was able to share Jesus with the man and introduce Him to the God He was looking for—the one true God, the God of the universe, the God who created all things. That man, in that place, at that time met God. As he prayed with Mark, his face filled with joy and peace, and that man would never be the same.

At the end of the day, I said to God, "You made my day, God!"

God said, "I knew I would."

"Thank You, God. It has been a very good day."

God said, "I told you it would be."

Ask the Father to speak to you today, and when He does, I pray you will be listening because He speaks to His sheep and they hear His voice.

PRAYER

How is your prayer life? Does it meet your expectations? Is God coming through for you? These questions will tell you a lot about your prayer life.

Is your priority each day as you pray to seek first the kingdom of God and His righteousness? What you utter in your prayer life reflects your relationship with God. Is your prayer life producing faith?

Prayer is not to be superficial but the deep desires of our heart—an earnest expectation that the God who made us can do all things and is waiting for our prayers because He wants to answer them.

Thinking about prayer one day after reading from Acts 12, my spirit moved me to not only tears but flat out crying. As I look at the church today, I see what Peter saw. In that passage it says the church prayed earnestly for Peter to be released from prison, but they were not praying expectantly for a miracle.

When Peter showed up, the woman who answered left Peter at the door and went to tell the others, and they didn't believe her. When we pray earnestly but without expectation that God will answer, it limits our view of God, it limits what we will pray for, and it limits the relationship we could have with Him.

Looking back on my life, it was when I prayed for the impossible, looking for a miracle, and expecting God to show up that some of the greatest moments of my life came. We serve the living God and the Creator of everything. That is you and me too.

He said to ask anything in Jesus' name and it will be given to you. Do you truly believe that? As for me and my house we do.

There have been times when it looked like I put God on the line. There were times when I said something that God could do that seemed quite impossible from the view of the person standing before me.

A girl who lived with us one summer said her family would never come to know Christ. Within a few months when my wife and I got to share the good news of Jesus and pray with them, God drew them to Himself and all of her family accepted Christ and the neighbor too.

Another said her husband had been bedridden for some time now, and she didn't know what to do. As I prayed, that man sat up with his arms lifted and said, "Praise Jesus, praise Jesus for He has healed me." God had indeed healed him.

Once when I was praying for a man with evil spirits, it seemed impossible that he would be set free. We had prayed for several hours and they didn't leave. At one point I was in tears, wondering why there was no success.

We continued to pray. At the point where we all seemed to be ready to give up, the Holy Spirit moved my heart to request the impossible. I said, "Jesus this is about You. It is not about us. We cannot do what You can do and Your name is above all names. Jesus, I don't know if You can do this, but we need You, Jesus!"

At that very moment, Jesus walked into the room. It was His Spirit. I could see His hands with holes in them. I could see His feet also with holes, and then as I gazed at His beautiful face, I could only look briefly and my head went down in humility, for I was in the presence of the Lord.

I was in awe and shocked as Jesus approached the man. I could see Jesus lean in toward him, and in an instant, the man we prayed hours for was totally free. We could hear a whoosh of the wind and then total and absolute silence.

One man in the room saw my face when all that happened. He said, "Did you just see Jesus?" I said yes. Another woman said, "No wonder it was over in an instant." When we finished that day the man who was freed told me what He had seen.

He said that he saw Jesus walk in and with a loving gentle smile reach out to him. Then the man said he put out his hand too and reached out to Jesus, and in a flash, all the evil in him was removed that day.

What do you think that day did for my prayer life? What do you think it did for my faith in God? My prayer life was radically changed because I saw how in an instant God will respond to our prayers, and how the impossible is not impossible for Him. For nothing is too hard for God, and He desires our prayers so that He can show us who He truly is, the One who was, who is, and who is to come: Jesus.

Jesus replied, "Truly I tell you, if you have faith and do not doubt, not only can you do what was done to the fig tree, but also you can say to this mountain, 'Go, throw yourself into the sea,' and it will be done. If you believe, you will receive whatever you ask for in prayer" (Matthew 21:21-22).

THIRTY MINUTES WITH GOD

A young man living with us told me how he was spending thirty minutes a day every single day with his girlfriend on the phone. She lives four hours from here. He told me how their relationship was growing and how he missed her. What I noticed was during this time his relationship with God was almost nonexistent, so I asked him a series of questions.

"How much time are you reading God's Word?"

"Not much," he said.

"How about praying to God and seeking direction for your life?"

Again, "Not much," he said.

My next question cut straight to the heart of the matter. "How do you expect the counsel and blessing that God has for you if you don't put time into the relationship with Him to know Him better?"

He could see his relationship with God was not good, but the relationship with his girlfriend had been strengthened by his time with her. So this chapter is about spending thirty minutes with God every day.

We are expected to read God's Word. It is good to set aside time every day to read from the Bible. Here is a verse to encourage you to do this.

Blessed is the one who reads aloud the words of this prophecy, and blessed are those who hear it and take to heart what is written in it, because the time is near (Revelation 1:3).

If we are studying the Bible every day and searching out its truths, we will grow in maturity as life goes forward. The following is a verse that describes this.

Do your best to present yourself to God as one approved, a worker who does not need to be ashamed and who correctly handles the word of truth (2 Timothy 2:15).

As we study and read every day, we can begin to prepare for a time when God will use His Word for His glory. Here is another verse to encourage us to be prepared.

How can a young person stay on the path of purity? By living according to your word. I seek you with all my heart; do not let me stray from your commands. I have hidden your word in my heart that I might not sin against you (Psalm 119:9-11).

When we are investing time into the relationship God wants with us, we will begin to see that we will be called to a life of faith. We will be challenged every day to live for Him. Here is another verse to encourage us in that.

Consequently, faith comes from hearing the message, and the message is heard through the word about Christ (Romans 10:17).

There is anticipation that God will speak to me each day when I get up and read my Bible. I long to know God better, to do His will, and to seek His face as I read His Word. I find myself in tears most days in my prayer room or at my store in my office as I study, memorize, and hide God's Word in my heart. Here is another passage speaking to the benefits of those times with God.

Keep this Book of the Law always on your lips; meditate on it day and night, so that you may be careful to do everything written in it. Then you will be prosperous and successful (Joshua 1:8).

Each day is another day to learn, to begin anew, to hold fast to the truth, and to live as Christ lived, for He has given us life. We should be giving more time to the One who gave us time to begin with and the One we will be with for all eternity. Wouldn't it be nice to know Him better before we meet Him face to face?

Is thirty minutes a day all the days of your life really that much to give? Today is a new day and can be the time you start opening His Word every single day for the rest of your life. I pray that you will make that commitment today.

He deserves our very best and one of the ways for Him to get the best is that we come to know Him better through His Word. When we think of eternity compared to thirty minutes, it is not such a big step.

TRUST

I am reminded of how God has brought me through so much. There have been times when my life seemed to be coming to an end, only to see God show just how much He loves me and is to be trusted.

In those times my mind wondered if God was going to come through for me. His quiet voice asked me, "Have I ever failed you, John?" The answer was and remains clearly, "No, God, You haven't." Never once in my life has He failed me."

When I have had a vision or dream come my way, it has always come true. Never has it not. God never does and never would lie. He is to be trusted with everything, including my very life.

Every nudge I get from Him has a purpose; every breath I breathe is so I can worship my King. My trust is in Him. The word "trust" means to hope confidently, to believe with assured anticipation. In other words, it means we put our life in His hands, knowing and believing it is for our own good.

Trust in the Lord with all your heart and lean not on your own understanding; in all your ways submit to him, and he will make your paths straight (Proverbs 3:5-6).

These verses teach us that when we trust in God, it will not be in a way that is always easy. When God says not to go by what you understand, He is saying He will call you to do things at times that may not make sense to you. In other words, His plans are not your plans, which is another verse quoted often.

If you trust God with your whole life, He gives you back a life that is worth living. I can sit here as I write and say that I have seen miracle after miracle and have heard the voice of God. I can tell you I was snatched from death's door, seen evil right in front of my face, and I did not flinch. God has taken me to places I would never have dreamed of going.

He has shown me love when I deserved none, and I have seen angels. During my 40 day fast, things were revealed to me about the path God is leading me down. I worked harder in those 40 days than when I am not fasting. God pushed me during that time to show how I could trust Him and Him alone, even for my very life.

I have seen God intervene on someone's behalf, before the prayer was even finished. I have seen God do amazing things to ensure success as I was serving others for Him and I had not even asked Him to do it. He just saw the need and supplied all I needed to get the job done. God is to be trusted with our lives, and thinking about it, we really shouldn't have that much trouble with it.

He knows us well. He created us. In Jeremiah 1:5 it says, "Before I formed you in the womb I knew you" and Matthew 10:30 says "even the hairs on your head are numbered." Those are some wonderful things that help us understand why we should be able to trust God.

He has a purpose for each of us and wants to give us a life pleasing to Him. And since God is love and loves us, that means He has our best interests in mind. If I were allowed the opportunity of encouraging anyone reading this, it would be to tell you on this day to chose to trust God with everything. I assure you that you will not go wrong.

When looking at people who trusted God, it is easy for

me to see Paul as one who trusted God beyond what most would probably do. You see although Paul was beaten, stoned, and left for dead, he never quit working for God. He was shipwrecked and had to swim to shore only to be bitten by a snake. Paul was imprisoned and ridiculed for his faith in God and proclamation that Jesus is Lord.

Paul took everything that came upon him and still was able to trust in the Lord's providence and know that what God says will happen, actually will. Paul was all in for God and he stayed the course, no matter where it went, knowing God was with him every step of the way, even unto death.

As I finish out the rest of my days, the hope of eternity with the One who created me grows stronger. My treasures are in heaven and my future is bright. My trust is in the One who knows me and knows in what way I can best be of use for Him on this earth. For His plans are to be trusted. If you haven't put your trust in the Lord, I would encourage you to do it today. It will be the best decision you will make in all your life.

YOUR STORY

Everyone has a story and those who know Christ have a story or testimony of what God has done for them. It is a story of how Christ delivered you from an eternity away from Him to an eternity where you will inherit heaven, and it is unique to only you.

No one else has walked the life you are living. How God brought you to Him is yours to share, and it should be something we share at every opportunity. You don't have to have all the scriptures memorized that you think you need to know. You don't need to have prayed hundreds of hours to be able to share it. You don't have to be a pastor, elder, or teacher to give your testimony. The great thing about your testimony is that you always have it with you. It is yours, and it is not a memory verse that can be forgotten. It is one of the greatest tools God has to use—the story of how His people were saved for His purpose because He loved them.

Moses was saved from the Nile and led God's people out of Egypt. God saved Joseph's family during the drought, showing us how God's plans are always best. Daniel was saved from the lion's den, and Noah was saved by God having him build an ark, and Shadrach, Meshach, and Abednego were saved from the fiery furnace by the Angel of the Lord who was with them. The list goes on and on, just like the generations since. God never stops bringing His people to Himself, and every generation since creation has had someone saved by God.

If you are reading this and are confused because you do not know the saving power of Jesus yet, let me encourage you to do that today. It is as simple as praying: "Father, forgive me for the wrongs I have done and come into my life, Jesus. I want You."

It is that easy for when we truly want a relationship with our Creator, we are given an opportunity to know Him. God will come in and save you from an eternity away from Him for "everyone who calls on the name of the Lord will be saved" (Romans 10:13). This verse guarantees that those who want to know God and call out for Him will be saved from eternal punishment.

Matthew 25:46 says the following: "And these will go away into eternal punishment, but the righteous into eternal life." This verse speaks of those who know God and those who don't, and how they will someday be separated—one to eternal light and one to eternal punishment.

The choice is yours to make, and that choice will have an impact on you for all eternity. For this life is fleeting, but eternity is forever. I pray that today is when you will ask Jesus to come into your life and allow Him to change it for the good.

Second Corinthians 5:17 says "Therefore, if anyone is in Christ, he is a new creation. The old has passed away; behold, the new has come."

In those words we are promised that there will be a change. I was a man of many addictions and now they are gone. Some were taken away in an instant and some as God taught me over a course of time, but the addictions, bad habits, and ugly life I lived are gone.

So that is part of my story and the question now is what

is yours? What are you going to do today? Are you going to accept God or reject Him? If you already know God, then what are you going to do for Him today?

You see even those choices are your story. How did you come to know Christ? What has He done for you since? How have you spread the good news of Jesus Christ since that day? All those things are a part of your story and until your last breath, the story of your life is still being played out. If your hope is in Christ and He has saved you, then you have a message to share.

Someone likely told you about Christ and helped you understand who He is, so as you are walking with God, you should be looking for opportunities to share what the Lord has and is doing in your life today. It is never too late to start spreading the good news to those who have yet to hear it.

May you on this day be the hands and feet of Jesus, walking as He walked and doing the amazing work He planned for you, before you were even born. May the precious name of Jesus be lifted high in all that you do and may His word encourage you greatly for He has saved you, so that you might live.

Blessings to you always!

About the Author

JOHN LANGER is an instrument that God has clearly chosen to use in unusual ways. He has had about 20 people move in with his family and has mentored well over 100 men and women toward a new or deeper relationship with God.

God is at the center of John's life and it shows. Even though he has traveled the world and been to almost every state in the US, he never stops giving credit to the great I AM.

John's passion is sharing Jesus with others. He has spoken in front of thousands and also shared with just one. His desire for others to know God is infectious and has drawn those with whom he fellowships to want a deeper relationship with God.

If you spend time with John, you would find him often in his prayer room for hours and hours just to get closer to the One he loves.

He is writing only because he believes God desires him to do so, and the access you have to these words are because God loves you and wants to know you better.

To contact the author, email him at
jlanger@venturecomm.net